Often Wrong, Never in Doubt

Donny Deutsch
with
Peter Knobler

Often Wrong, Never in Doubt

Unleash the Business Rebel Within

Collins

An Imprint of HarperCollinsPublishers

HarperCollins books may be purchased for educational, business,
or sales promotional use. For information, please write to:
Special Markets Department, HarperCollins Publishers,
10 East 53rd Street, New York, New York 10022.

FIRST EDITION

Designed by Nick Ferguson

Library of Congress Cataloging-In-Publication has been
applied for.

ISBN-10:   0-06-056718-X
ISBN-13: 978-0-06-056718-7
05   06   07   08   09   DIX!/RRD   10   9   7   6   5   4   3   2   1

To my dad, who did the hard part.

—D.D.

For Daniel and Jane

—P.K.

Acknowledgments

I'd like to thank my partner in crime, Peter Knobler, whose wisdom, judgment, genius, and good humor made the process of writing this book not only bearable but a lot of fun.

My editor at HarperCollins, Marion Maneker, a smart and perceptive man, made the book better than it had any right to be. All the people at HarperCollins, especially Joe Tessitore, Libby Jordan, George Bick, Paul Olsewski, Larry Hughes, and Edwin Tan, kept making it better and better.

My managing partners at Deutsch Inc.—Kathy Delaney, Val DiFebo, Cheryl Greene, Eric Hirshberg, Linda Sawyer, Mike Sheldon—and partners Bobbi Casey/Howell, Peter Gardiner, Fred Rubin, Nina Werner, and Jeffrey Wolf were all extremely helpful. Reliving stories and memories with Linda, Val, Kathy, Mike, and Eric made the past present again. Cheryl did an inspired edit on the Brand Ethos Model chapter. Our senior vice president/director of business development, Mike Duda gave good time, energy, and ideas to the project.

Special thanks to Linda Sawyer, who not only has been by my side as a partner and friend, but who went over every word of the book with me to make sure I didn't get myself in trouble, something she's been doing for the last fifteen years.

My wonderful assistants, Jennifer Ratchford, Stephanie Jones, Lisa Bass, and Morgan Witkin (aka the Deutschettes)—not only helped shepherd this book but make every minute of my day better and richer.

All my dear friends, who know who they are, put up with my craziness during the writing of this book (and always).

I also want to thank everybody who has ever worked at Deutsch. You helped make it the best agency that ever existed on the planet.

Wayne Kabak, my agent, good friend, and consigliere, got this book going. Esther Newberg helped put Peter Knobler and me together.

Nadine Wolf and Joycelyn Furginson transcribed with great enthusiasm.

To my sister, Amy, who has always been there for me. Special thanks to my mom, who always gave me loving pushes. To Chelsey who brings a special light to my life. To Stacy who always has a place in my heart.

And finally to my dad—the man who started this whole thing—his example of grace, dignity, hard work, and heart have provided me the ultimate role model for success. He read every word and did his best to keep me out of harm's way, something he's been working at for the last 47 years.

Contents

The Business World

Your Own World

The Next World

The Real World

The Self-Entitlement Injection Theory

The key to success is not purely who's the smartest, who's the best, but also who can say with conviction, "I deserve it." The entire concept is wrapped up in one phrase:

Why not me?

Why not me? You can't just say it, you've got to own it.

In order to pitch $10-million accounts, you've got to say, "We should be pitching." Who's going to get that $10-million account? Why not me? Why stop at $10 million? Or $100-million accounts? Why not me? Whenever I say those words to people, they laugh. They hear their own wheels turning, they realize how far they are from acting on that kind of question, and they laugh.

How'd I figure this out? Richie Kirshenbaum taught me without even knowing it.

Richie Kirshenbaum was the first guy I ever hired. He was maybe six months out of Syracuse University, working for a small agency called Korey Kay & Partners. If I was thirty he was twenty-six, a clever, funny, fast-talking guy. He had a lot of fun headlines in his book, so I hired him.

We got along great. I was the main front guy; Richie did a lot of the writing. It seemed to be working.

After two years David Deutsch Associates was starting to make some inroads. We weren't seen as one of the hot shops, the sexy, bigger-name creative agencies like Chiat/Day or Ammirati Puris. We didn't have a lot of notoriety; we were this little boutique print house that had been around for fifteen years that was making more noise than we used to. We were a small, high-end creative shop and we were known as a small, high-end creative shop.

Richie could have been a Borscht Belt comedian. He was great with one-liners, a fast-talking storyteller not unlike early Woody Allen. A typical neurotic, self-deprecating Long Island Jewish guy. I thought of him as my protégé, my sidekick, and we had a lot of fun together. When, after two years, he left to go work at J. Walter Thompson, I understood. He was going to a bigger place, more money, more responsibility. Time to move on. No big deal. We remained friends.

About six months later I heard that Richie was going to start his own agency with some guy I'd never heard of. I laughed and dismissed it. "Boy, he's certainly not equipped to start an ad agency." Lot of balls, that kid. "Oh yeah," I said to myself, "that'll last a week."

The first campaign they did was for Kenneth Cole shoes. Very controversial, political ads. Not about shoes at all; about the attitude behind the shoes. It was an immediate hit. They did a couple more controversial campaigns. In those days everyone read Bernice Kanner's advertising column in *New York* magazine. One week Kanner wrote a two-page spread about how Richie Kirshenbaum was running the agency of the moment. Here was this little *pischer,* a couple of months into it, he'd done a few nifty ads and positioned himself, and *he had the hot agency!*

I got insanely jealous.

That lasted about a minute. Then my jealousy turned to *"Ah ha!"* Wait a second, I figured; here's a guy who I actually know. Richie and I have worked side by side. I think I'm smarter than this guy. I think I'm a harder worker. I think I've got a bigger set of balls. I lived with this guy for two years; now I'm reading about him. What's wrong with this picture? How did this happen? What's Richie got that I haven't got that's making him so hot?

No bells started flashing, no lightbulb went on over my head, but it didn't take long for me to figure it out. Richie had a fully developed sense of entitlement. He'd clearly said to himself, "Why shouldn't I have the next hot agency?" Richie was looking to make his mark on the world. His answer was, "I should."

What hit me was that Richie went into his new company saying, "We're going to be the next hot agency," and worked back from there. "What do I have to do?" He'd figured, "If I want a hot agency, I've got to do a specific type of work that not only pleases the client but is also going to get a certain kind of attention."

Me? I wasn't even dreaming that David Deutsch Associates would get written up in *New York*. We had been grinding all along but never thought it was possible. Million-dollar clients? Out of our league. If someone had asked me, "Why shouldn't you have the next hot agency?" I'd have had every answer in the world except the right one. Richie Kirshenbaum showed me I was wrong. Why *couldn't* we do work like I was reading about? That could be us. That *should* be us. We could pitch anybody. But first we had to own it. If we wanted to be written about, we'd first have to create the kind of ads that garner attention. Why not me? From then on I started to do ads that would make waves.

It also didn't hurt that I now had someone driving me crazy. It's good, in business, to have someone to shoot at, someone you want to knock off his pedestal. Makes it personal. I didn't hate Richie— I actually had a lot of affection for him—but I hated his success; we were still bigger, but he was the agency of the moment, the agency du jour. He had no business getting the kind of attention that was coming at him. I used that as a tool. My guiding principle became: Why Not Me?

Unless you're an exceptional human being from the get-go—which most people, including myself, are not—our entire social system is basically about putting people in boxes. School, in particular, should be educating children to their possibilities but instead serves just to standardize them. For my whole academic career, my behavior was "unsatisfactory," and my self-control was "unsatisfactory" because I had a creative mind and it wandered. Dreams are vital—all I did was daydream—but I got penalized for mine. The world is littered with people who've been shoved back into boxes and didn't have the personal firepower to fight their way out. Maybe some kids in fourth grade are told, "You're exceptional"—maybe their parents tell them constantly, which can add a whole other set of problems—but most are told to know their place. My parents knew I was bright and had leadership qualities. They had no clue as to my creativity.

When asked, I tell people to *find* their place. I don't have children, but if I did, I wouldn't tell them, "You can be president of the United States." I'd tell them, "Follow your dream. You're entitled to your dream. If your dream is to be president of the United States, then why not you?"

Inside all of us, somewhere, is a dream. But no one is going to tap you on the shoulder, pluck you out of the chorus, and make you a star. First you've got to make the conscious decision to pursue that dream. You've got to put it in Drive. Want to be a chef? An investment banker? What do you have to do to get there? What's the first step? Take it!

The older you become, the more your dreams get rationalized, the more you come to terms with your compromises; you know the corners you've cut better than anybody. In a Jewish family, what are we brought up to want to be? Doctor, lawyer. Make a good living. It's a pretty narrow box. We weren't brought up to be president or a movie star, or to cure cancer. Most people want to please—our parents, our teachers, our clergymen—so rather than pursuing our own dreams, we follow a compendium of theirs. That rarely works. The happiest people are the ones who follow their own dreams most closely. The day your dream dies, a little part of you dies. And all of us want to live forever.

Pick your own dream. There are 20,000 advertising copywriters in New York City right now. If I polled them, I'm absolutely positive that 19,990 would say they deserve to be a creative director. "I'm working for them, I'm smarter than they are, I do all the work . . ." Every one of them. But until they say, "I should have that job, if not here, someplace else—and here's why," they'll stay at their desks and begrudgingly meet their deadlines.

On one level or another, those people either don't think they deserve it or don't have the skills. If they did, they would make it happen. The math on that equation is, having the skills is necessary but doesn't guarantee success. For every person with the stuff, the one out of a hundred who goes to a very rarefied place is the one who says, "Why not me?" and goes for it.

Fuckin' Richie Kirshenbaum. I've got him to thank for all this.

The Queens Logic Formula: How I Got This Way

My particular strengths were street smarts, intuition, people skills, salesmanship. In honors class I was the village idiot.

I was always a good athlete, not a great athlete. My mouth made me better. Whether it was touch football or basketball or baseball, in the streets of Hollis Hills, Queens, I was always a six with a ten mouth. I was born at the end of November, so I was considerably younger than the rest of the kids in my class. When you're eight years old, that half a year makes a big difference. Today those kids are put in the following grade. Not me. So I had some talking to do.

Talk of money was not in my universe. To my parents' credit, growing up in my neighborhood we never put a premium on money. Life in Hollis Hills was the opposite of our nouveau riche Long Island suburban neighbors'; there was a lot of money in Hollis Hills but people lived under their means. It was never discussed. My father made a very nice living, we lived in a lovely house, and had all the advantages of middle- to upper–middle-class life. I went to the finest summer camps, I was given pretty much anything I asked for, I wanted for nothing. I didn't discriminate between my friends who lived in a garden apartment, the projects, or a Victorian home. Very low-key. There was no money food chain. The premium was put on achievement, on being a success. That was important.

But Hollis Hills was this little enclave in the larger mass of Queens. At home I lived this privileged life; during the day I went to Van Buren High School where I was exposed to much more of the schoolyard mentality. I had the best of both worlds. I had it really good.

My father worked in advertising. He had worked as a creative director at Ogilvy & Mather, one of the top agencies in the city, before opening his own shop, David Deutsch Associates. He told me, "Find something you love." My mom gave me the same advice, but like so many Jewish mothers at the time, having been brought up to respect men with good jobs, she wanted me to be a professional. As I grew up they could have recognized that I had a more creative bent, but like a lot of kids, I was told, "That's fun and all, but . . . doctor, lawyer, accountant." For me, there was no alternative.

At Martin Van Buren High School there were gifted, or honors, classes and then classes for the regular *schtummy*-head student body. Because it was important to get into a good college, to achieve, I started out with the honors students. Nerds. I'm not saying they all had pocket protectors, but they were the kids in the science fairs, not necessarily the great athletes or the most popular, the kids who defined themselves by being great students. That was their reason to be.

I'd always thought I was pretty smart, but in honors class I was the village idiot. I was the guy who cracked the jokes, the one who when called upon wasn't paying attention. I tried. From the first day of school I told myself, "I'm going to pay attention. I'm going to pay attention!" And if you looked at my notebook, you would see for the first two paragraphs I would take really nice notes. Then would follow doodles of gladiators and dinosaurs. I think if I was a schoolkid today, I would be diagnosed with Attention Deficit Disorder. You could actually see my mind drifting.

Academics wasn't my bailiwick. I didn't like to work and I was always looking for the angles. Starting in elementary school, I would come home with B's and B+'s on my report cards, accompanied by comments like, "Donny is a wonderful boy. If he worked harder, he could be a very good student." That was death. When my friends came home with the same reports, their folks were perfectly happy. Not mine. I got saddled with the P-word. My mom was a teacher. She would challenge me, "As long as you fool around you will not live up to your potential!"

My parents and I still argue about this thirty-five years later. The report card said I was capable of more, therefore I should have been doing more. They have a legitimate point. But the American academic system is not set up for kids who are not linear thinkers. Academics is about linear thinking and memory. Given my IQ, my creative mind, my undiagnosed ADD, the fact that I liked to fool around, that I was a little rambunctious and couldn't sit still—I was doing the best I could do. That *was* my potential!

For motivation, my mom didn't make me read a book; between sixth and twelfth grades, she prevented me from going to basketball games with my friends, she wouldn't let me go out on the weekends. That hurt. A lot. What did I do instead? I watched TV and smoked pot. (I started smoking marijuana in eighth grade. I was never a big druggie in high school, though the '70s were well underway and all kinds of pills and apothecary were easily available. Just a pot smoker, and never during school hours. There were plenty of guys doing much worse.)

In ninth grade I did well enough grade-wise, 85s and 87s, but a lot of it was because of my personality. I was the only non-nerd in the class and I charmed the teachers.

I never defined myself as a student. If you'd asked me, "Donny, do you want to get A's or do you want to be popular?" I'd always have gone with being the center of the circle. I didn't have a master plan; I knew I wanted to achieve something but I didn't know what it was. I just wanted to be good in sports and I wanted to have a lot of friends. It took the school administration a year to figure that out and in tenth grade they transferred me out of honors and into the general population.

Van Buren was one of those huge stone institutions that looked like a prison. You've got to wonder, when they built these places, what they could have been thinking. Every day we walked into the clink, and in some respects it lived up to its looks.

There were two really tough groups: the greasers, who we called "hitters," and a hard bunch of blacks. I was more afraid of the hitters. Van Buren was so big they couldn't fit everybody into the school building for the normal school day, so they had sessions; the freshman class did the standard 9-to-3 and walked up and down special staircases, while the tenth graders went from 12:30 to 5:30 and the eleventh and twelfth graders started at 7:40 and got out at 12:30. My second week there, some guy put a knife to my neck and said, "Give me your bus pass." I was really quick. I said, "Here." Done.

You couldn't go to the bathroom; that was where the real thugs hung out; if you didn't have your wits about you, you'd get the shit beat out of you. A lot of guys went through four years and didn't go to the bathroom. But sooner or later I had to take a piss, so I made sure I knew one of the real thugs and somehow I did something right by him. I don't remember what it was. Chris Lang, I think his name was. Long hair. Gave me a cultural pass into the bathroom. Basically saved my life.

I learned pretty quickly that if you walked like you weren't scared of people, that did it, the tough ones would go pick on an easier mark. At the end of the day, people prey on what's easiest. I'm afraid of nature, I won't jump out of an airplane for anything in the world, but with something concrete I'm fine. I'll walk through the toughest neighborhood at two in the morning, no problem.

The only time I really thought I was going to get my ass handed to me I was coming home late and walked out of the subway station and there, standing around, were maybe a hundred sixteen-year-old punks looking for trouble. I could see them pointing. I wished they were a couple of years older so they would know better, but they were just bad guys and I could tell I was going to either get hit on for my wallet or get the crap beat out of me. So I started walking toward them, cursing wildly. "Fuck you! Fuck you assholes. Fuck all of you!" I was almost spitting, flailing my arms. Didn't make eye contact—didn't make that mistake—but I kept moving, kept cursing.

Nobody screws with a crazy person. I started to laugh and one of them said, "That guy is fucking nuts." The crowd parted like they were letting a fighter through to the ring and I never stopped, just kept on going. I lived to tell.

As a boy I played in the street all the time and I never picked on other kids. I hated when kids would cry and I always stuck up for them. I'm not saying I made the nerdiest guy my best friend, but my stomach always churned when kids were mean to each other. I tended to be a leader in our group and when someone was getting picked on, I was usually able to say, "Aaah come on, man, leave Billy alone."

With my big mouth I should have gotten into a lot of fights, and there were plenty of times I thought I was going to get beat up, but I was lucky.

There was a tough kid in my neighborhood named Curtis Pflug. I was with a girl I was dating and I said something about him, and he and this other beefy guy, Steve Traccarico, started pushing me, calling me out in front of her, trying to get me to put up my fists. I wouldn't engage; I knew if I did, I was going to get pum-

meled. They taunted me but still I wouldn't go after them. The fact
that my girl was there to hear it made it even harder.

For years afterward that really stuck in my head. A young guy
struggles with that. Would it have been better to get my ass kicked
or say, "Screw it, you guys are assholes" and walk away? Either way,
the ego's getting a shot. It wasn't until a decade later that I could
look back and feel I'd done the right thing.

I only got in one fistfight in my life. When I was around twelve,
there was a redheaded kid who was kind of a dweeb and out in the
schoolyard it came to blows. I got him in a headlock and was banging his head on the concrete. My first fight and I was winning. Finally I let him up and the guys were cheering and the kid ran
home crying. I felt so bad afterward that I went to his house—
didn't tell anybody about it—and apologized to him. Winning the
fight didn't make me feel particularly good but apologizing made
me proud.

So in my tenth grade homeroom finally I was in my natural cultural subset. I looked around and said, quite happily, "I'm not the
only fuckup in the room anymore!"

There were real thugs in my classes. Kids who would set the
room on fire, sit in the back stoned all day, tell the teachers to go
fuck themselves. They didn't want to be there; they were sitting in
class at Van Buren because even the lowest common denominator
in society went to high school. You couldn't *not* go; it was the law,
you went to school or you went to jail. Soon enough. These guys
ended up working nights somewhere, or being criminals. These
weren't young men who were going to college; they weren't on
track for post-graduate degrees; they were on track for work-
release.

I felt perfectly comfortable.

The maximum a general-studies student could get in a class
was 92; that's if you got everything right, a 92. One hundreds
were not on the grade curve for us; the level of instruction and

intelligence topped out at 92. So I cracked my jokes, doodled my doodles, got my 92s. To a lot of these delinquents, I was the nerd.

The only class I didn't have any trouble paying attention in, the one I actually looked forward to attending, was speech. This wasn't elocution, it was drama and presentation, and it was fun. I'd write speeches and get up in front of everybody and orate. Speech class played to my skills, and I played it to the hilt. It wasn't like going to school.

Every springtime the New York State education department conducts a standardized test called the Regents exam for all New York public high school students in each of the major academic fields. Some schools focus their curriculum all year on this one test; doesn't matter what you actually learn in class, just do well on the Regents. Fail it and you're left back. Fail enough of them and you don't get your degree. It's the New York State standard of excellence.

In tenth grade I took the social studies Regents. This test wasn't simply a multiple-choice exam; it incorporated essays in which the student was required to make an argument and back it up persuasively with facts. I was able to use my writing skills, my communication skills, the abilities I had shown in speech class.

The Kid from *Deliverance* got a 98! It was the highest grade received by anyone in all of Van Buren.

My teacher, Mrs. Schneider, was so proud. She probably didn't have a kid in any of her classes who got over a 70 on anything, and here a boy from the retard class beat every honors student in the school.

Something went off in my head: I do have some intellect; I just achieve in a different setting than the standard. I put a reverse spin on potential. Maybe potential had a correlation with comfort level. When I had been put in a social environment that was all about studying, I didn't fit in and I had sunk to the bottom of the class. When I had been put in a class in which I felt I belonged so-cially, I was able to access and use the best of my mind. Maybe if schools put their students where they felt most comfortable, they would flourish. It sure worked for me.

A lot of good it did me. Now that it was established that I was, indeed, a student, I was expected to study. I continued to get my general-education 92s. I can't say I thrived. I don't think I have a great IQ. My SAT scores were good but not groundbreaking, around 1200. My particular strengths were street smarts, intuition, people skills, salesmanship. They're hard to quantify. What I did learn was that I was not an academic.

Still, I had a good time at Van Buren senior year. I had a bunch of guys and girls I would hang out with. Most of our crowd did well in school; we were hip and fun and social and popular. We weren't the renegades, we weren't the potheads. We were good kids. We'd go to parties or to the movies or just hang at people's houses. It was a very self-contained Queens world. We didn't drift out to Long Is-land; we only rarely went into the city. (We lived in Queens, which is just as much part of New York City as Brooklyn or Manhattan, but Manhattan was "the city" and we didn't go there often.) Every once in a long while a few of my buddies and I, including Steve Martini and Stuie Cantor, would hit Forty-second Street—the real Forty-second Street, the dirty Forty-second Street. We'd go in some joint, and down one aisle there would be peep shows and up on this grungy platform a guy would be fucking a woman. Very bizarre.

We weren't a big drinking crowd and we didn't go to the bars in the city; we'd come home and end up at our local diner. It sat across the street from the Creedmoor state mental hospital, so to us it was the Looney Tunes Diner.

I played every sport every season in the street. (I didn't even try to go out for the school teams. When you go to a New York City public high school, a white boy doesn't make the basketball team unless he's six foot ten; though if I'd gone to Roslyn High School on Long Island, I probably would have started.) Van Buren had no football team. The soccer team was all Hispanic.

I was very happy. I loved my friends, I finally loved school. I was elected class president, which may have been a big deal in other high schools but at Van Buren it didn't mean shit to most students. As president, I gave a speech on stage and accepted the diploma on behalf of the Class of '75. (I was the only student who actually physically received a diploma on the stage; there were so many kids in the school that we couldn't all go up and get one—it would have been a five-hour graduation.)

Senior year was so good, in fact, that when it came time for college, I didn't want to go.

I was accepted by the University of Pennsylvania—in June 1975, off the waiting list. I think I was the last guy they admitted. If there were 1,700 incoming students in my class, I had the credentials to be number 1,700. I was terrified about going to college, where you really had to work. I was terrified of leaving home. If I'd had any sense, I would have applied to the S.I. Newhouse School of Public Communications at Syracuse, used the real skills I did have and loved it.

I didn't belong in an Ivy League school. Ivy League schools are for students, high-achieving academic students. I didn't think I could compete with those people in that world. Didn't mean I couldn't compete with those people in the real world. Didn't mean I didn't have a lot of skills they didn't have.

I arrived at Penn for orientation and, first of all, there were WASPs. I'd been surrounded by Jews and Italians my whole life; I barely knew a WASP existed, had never seen the critter before. I quickly found out that, as smart as they were, the guys at Penn didn't have their wits about them. Most of the friends I made had gone to either all-Jewish schools on Long Island or all-WASP schools in Connecticut. They hadn't gone to tough, integrated, four-thousand-student prison facilities. They came from very insulated, homogeneous worlds and had never been exposed to the street. They hadn't played in my kind of schoolyards. Not a one would have lasted a minute in the bathroom at Van Buren. No matter how bright they were, I couldn't wait to play cards with these guys, take their money, drink their beer, and steal their girlfriends.

(If they had girlfriends. At Penn there were five guys to every girl and each coed was uglier than the next. Sometime that fall I went and visited my buddy Perry Schorr at Syracuse, where the ratio was three-to-one and the babes were just steaming. I said, "Wait a minute. I got the 92 average; Perry got an 80 and he's having the time of his life. Who's the winner? What's the lesson here?")

I quickly found a circle of friends—that was never a problem. But in the classroom I had to find a way get myself through. I couldn't go back; high school was over. I worked as hard as I had to and got a 3.0 grade point average freshman year.

I had been the last one admitted to Penn, but at that time in the mid '70s, it was easy to transfer into the Wharton School, the jewel of the University of Pennsylvania system, where students are given "the opportunity to focus on an integrated curriculum of business and liberal arts." A place, its brochure says, "where you can explore your options."

I determined, for one year, to put my nose to the grindstone. I had spent most of my four years at Van Buren and freshman year at Penn not really working, on the assumption that I could do the work if I really wanted to. So now I really wanted to. I wanted to prove something to myself.

I didn't realize it while it was happening, but sophomore year at Wharton I learned how to think. While I took courses and learned finance, what they taught me that was more important was, "Okay, this is your means to an end." Wharton was all about getting from A to B first and best. Wharton was not about academia; Wharton was about success. I definitely liked that.

I worked hard for a while, really banged it out. In the second semester of sophomore year my GPA was 3.8 (4 A's and a B). But the better I did, the higher my grades, the more I got bored. I challenged myself, and when I won the challenge, I put it aside. What could I do now?

Second semester junior year I smoked pot and listened to Peter Frampton. During the day I'd watch *Happy Days* reruns, then go down on campus to Locust Walk and hang out. I'd go to class, maybe play some sports, play some pinball, work out, go to dinner. Always out and about. We partied hard, had a lot of fun, and were pretty much waste products, my core group of friends and I. As for school, I waited till the last two weeks, crammed all night every night and somehow got by.

Time came for me to graduate. I didn't take the summer off and travel to Europe; I'd been on vacation for a couple of years now.

I could have worked with my father. For most of the '60s he had been executive art director at McCann-Erickson. In those days, all agency art directors reported to the executive AD; my father held a job of significant importance. In 1969 my dad had been hired away by Ogilvy & Mather to be one of six creative directors, unusual because Ogilvy didn't make a practice of hiring outside the firm. Clearly they respected his work; however, my father and David Ogilvy never hit it off.

Ogilvy, the man, had very particular rules concerning creativity. Today, I find those kinds of restrictions foolish and counterproductive. Back then, it was just Ogilvy's way of doing things. In particular, one of his guiding advertising principles was: Never Run an Advertisement with Reverse Type. My father and he had many run-ins, one of the biggest when my dad showed him an ad with white type on a black background. Ogilvy made things very difficult for my dad—years later my father told me many stories of what a son of a bitch the guy was—and eventually things didn't work out. It's a shame when business geniuses bully their executives.

David Ogilvy has a rarefied reputation in advertising, but he wasn't a very nice man. He was known to have once walked by a secretary's desk, found it too messy for his liking, and with a sweep of his arm, pushed everything onto the floor. He berated his employees. That's just mean-spirited. My father is the finest, most talented, hardest-working person there is, and maybe I'm just a son sticking up for his dad, but that shows me something, the kind of person who would bully my dad.

Disgusted with so much of the mediocre work and internal politics of the big agencies, my father gathered a few freelance jobs, rented an office with an art director, and in 1969 opened his own shop, David Deutsch Associates. He felt that a small boutique could do consistently better work. When I got out of school, I chose not to join him. Dad had a great reputation as creative director's creative director, and his agency was known for its high-end design and elegant, manicured work. A genius of twenty-two, I said, "It's print, it's boring." I saw his business as tedious, its attitude as dry and limited, and I walked away.

Wharton turned out great business graduates and many companies sent recruiters to campus to sign up fresh talent for the coming year. Ogilvy & Mather sent several executives to interview prospective employees. Steve Humphrey was the senior executive who interviewed me. (Why did I consider working for them when they had fired my father? Good question. Ogilvy was at the top of the advertising food chain and I thought it was a good idea to start at the top. My father concurred.) Humphrey was a very straitlaced man, right out of Darien, Connecticut. He asked, "What are your outside interests?"

I had absolutely no overview. I wasn't trying to be clever; I literally did not know any better. I told him, "Chicks and basket-ball."

Humphrey fell off his chair. "Time out!" He stopped the interview. Pulled in his colleague who was busy interviewing in the adjoining room, an Ogilvy executive named Patty Deneroff, and said, "You've got to hear this."

I got that job.

Ogilvy & Mather was big-time. It had all the buzz of a growing, high-visibility organization. I had been in and out of half a dozen people's offices during the course of my interview there, and I showed up for my first day on my $15,000-a-year job and got a $1,000 signing bonus.

I had gone shopping; I wanted to look the part of an advertising executive. I went to Syms, where "an educated consumer is our best customer." I guess I wasn't their best. I showed up for work in a tan polyester Calvin Klein suit and Florsheim pleather shoes. I don't even know how they let me through the door.

What could the gentlemen at Ogilvy have thought? I walked in and saw all these WASPy guys dressed in Paul Stuart outfits, braces, straight-tipped or wing-tipped shoes, shirts with contrasting collars, foulard ties. And there I was looking like a *gavone*, like I should have been on Seventh Avenue.

I was very impressed and taken with Ogilvy's white-shoe dress code. I quickly went to Church's and bought the proper shoes; I bought braces; I adopted the look.

At Ogilvy everything was red. The walls, the carpet, the doors. The place was a maze of hallways and rows of little offices, each with a person's name on the door, each door closed. Low ceilings. The area in which I was seated was an open area, a bullpen; my little cubicle backed up against someone else who was doing much the same job. I was on the General Foods floor.

My first boss was a chain-smoking, hard-drinking, early-thirties account executive. I got the sense that he had "old money" and was spending his days at Ogilvy simply because he wanted to. After work he headed straight for the martinis. Very affected Darien vocal inflection. Southampton lockjaw. A real WASP. He was my boss on the Maxwell House coffee account. *Good to the very last drop.* I got a memo the morning of that first day saying that we were all meeting for a Maxwell House "donut exploratory." How nice, I thought; refreshments. What a thoughtful company.

I walked in ready to dunk and found that what they called a "donut" was a product demonstration. (A commercial's "donut," I came to understand, is the part in which the product is demonstrated.) This particular presentation was not in finished form; it was animatics, in which the art department moves renderings of the product in a general approximation of how the ad will look; later the agency tests the ad in focus groups and gets a sense of how the public will respond. I was in a room with the Ogilvy Maxwell House brain trust and they were all seized with a passion over how best to explain to the public the benefit of the thirteen ounces of coffee that would now be puffed up and filling the sixteen-ounce can.

When you don't know anything, sometimes you see things extremely clearly. Never mind the duplicity of shortchanging the consumer; I watched twenty people wrestle over the tradecraft and minutiae of how to present this five-second demonstration so the client would accept it. They were absurdly involved, voices were raised, personalities were clashing, and I thought, "There is really something stupid about this."

Later that day I was brought in to meet the management supervisor who was running the Maxwell House business. I figured, "Fine, I'll meet the guy." For the people making the introduction, even entering his vestibule was a big deal.

I walked in and his entire office was lined with Coffee Cans from All Nations. Hundreds and hundreds of antique coffee cans from around the globe. Russian coffee cans, Hungarian coffee cans, Peruvian coffee cans. Sri Lankan, Colombian, the exotic Kona. If there was a wine cellar for the coffee connoisseur, this was it. This guy was truly Mr. Coffee. He sat me down and intoned, "You know, Donny, nobody knows coffee like I know coffee. I've done this for thirteen years."

I could feel the thought bubble appear over my head. I was hoping he couldn't see it. In this bubble were two ideas. Number one: "What an asshole!" And number two: "Wait. So I'm going to kill myself for the next thirteen years for this?!"

I was a charming new critter to these corporate people. I didn't fit their mold; my interview had proved that, which was why they had hired me. Later I saw a memo that had been distributed about me, which said, in substance, "Seems as if we've got a real good worker with Donny. He's lively and energetic. Let's make sure we get him on track." Still, the first day I was there I was told, "Don't talk. Don't say anything. Just listen and learn." That made sense; I had to get a feel for how things were done at my new company.

At Ogilvy there were creatives and there were business guys. Coming out of Wharton, I was a business guy. They made me an assistant account executive and for the next eight months they pushed me. For all their intentions to use my youth and enthusiasm, my superiors gave me budgets to recap, numbers to crunch, reports to write. Not that I'd thought I was going to walk in and create new worlds, but I could just as easily have been working for an accounting firm.

On my first or second day I was introduced to the assistant brand manager of the Maxwell House account, an attractive woman on the client side whose name I recall as Barbara Lawrence. The next day I called Barbara and said, "Let's have lunch." I was trying to bond with the client. Within hours the hubbub got back to me.

"You're not supposed to do that!"

"Why not? I'm an ad guy; I'm supposed to take the client out to lunch."

"She's a level above you. That's not done at your level; you don't have direct client contact."

I thought, "Hey, wait a second, I've been watching *Bewitched,* this is what you do!" "Oh no," I was told quite firmly. "Only at the next level do you actually have direct client contact."

Huh?

I thought this was incredibly silly. They didn't, and what they thought counted. And as I crunched my numbers and wrote my reports, I found a lot more that just didn't make any sense.

I was beyond bored. I took to turning my chair around, standing on it, and chatting over the cubicle wall with my bullpen neighbor. That wasn't done, either.

They moved me around, trying to find a product or job that suited me, and every new person I worked for asked me off their business. I didn't learn any advertising secrets, but what did become clear was that I could never exist in a corporate culture. It was all about thinking in boxes, never peering around their sides or over their tops. I tried. And they tried. The people at Ogilvy were wonderful to me and really made every attempt to have it work. It was me who didn't make it easy for them. After a few months I took to leaving the office during the day and just roaming around the city. I'd duck into Chock full o' Nuts for a nutted cheese sandwich, then come back to my three little half-walls and my papers.

If I wasn't doing any good at Ogilvy, I was learning about corporate culture. Being in a business environment, seeing how people talk, how they conduct themselves, the way they walk, the interaction, the caste systems—I had never seen that before. And I knew I didn't want to be in this kind of a culture again. Which was a difficult piece of information. Ogilvy & Mather was a tremendously successful business and I had failed there. Where, and in what environment, could I succeed? I had no idea. If this was how corporations operated, I'd have to create my own.

Finally, after about nine months, I went into Steve Humphrey's office and said, "I don't think this is working out. I should have taken some time off after school; I need to go find myself." I'm amazed they hadn't fired me before then. I certainly deserved it. I was immature, I was stupid, I wasn't ready for the job. I've got nobody to blame but myself. I was a fuckup.

How to Get in the Door When the Door's Not Open

The definition of insanity is cueing the same behavior and expecting a different outcome.

Change doesn't happen organically; it doesn't happen by itself. People wait for change like they're waiting for a bus. People want things to happen, they want to get farther down the road, but that bus ain't coming; it's only when they go out and flag a ride that they get where they want to go.

After I blew out of Ogilvy, I went out west to fool around. Stayed in Los Angeles with my friend Steve Martini. Got on TV on the *Match Game* in my polyester suit. Spent six months doing nothing, came back. I really didn't have anything in mind. I was turned off to advertising, but my father said, "You want to give it a shot and join me?" I did.

I had a degree from Wharton, so I joined the agency in 1983

not as a creative but as an account executive. Our big clients were Ambi Skin Tone, a skin cream for African-Americans, and Letts of London diaries. Letts paid us a $3,000-a-month retainer and we designed their catalog. I was sitting in a meeting with two of their executives and they began to plot out the business. "We should put the blue-striped diary here and the black one on page two . . ." They were so serious, jumping around the room, very excited about the work they were doing. I broke out laughing.

"What are you laughing at?" one asked me.

"You guys take this really seriously." I just didn't see how anyone could get excited about anything in business.

I hated the ad business. I thought I was a creative sort and I'd see my dad in his room, working with his partners, trying to come up with creative ideas for Oneida Silversmiths. I wanted to get involved in their conversations, but he said, "Nah, we really need you on the account side."

Even on that side I wasn't on top of things. I was working but my heart and soul weren't into it. I would go to meetings and handle clients, but I wasn't putting myself out. I was the boss's jerk-off son and I think my father recognized that. He really cared about his company and I didn't. "You know what?" he finally told me. "You're not taking this seriously. Take a walk. Find work you love. Get the fuck outta here." I'm sad to say he was right.

I stumbled around for six months, sold Gitano jeans at a flea market, really didn't know what I wanted to do. I had been accepted at George Washington Law School when my dad decided to sell his business. He got an offer from an agency in Philadelphia, Spiro, that wanted a presence in New York. My father and his partners were in their mid-fifties; he was going to sell and stay on working there for another five years and then retire. My dad had been running the place for fourteen years. He'd had enough.

I hadn't. I knew this was a moment and an opportunity that arrived only rarely, and not being a complete moron, I also knew this was not a *schmatte* business that could easily be passed down from generation to generation; this was a business based on the brains and skills of one person, my father. I also had the strong feeling that my father wasn't ready. I sat with my dad and told him, "You don't want to sell it. Don't sell it. I want to come back but . . . I'm not an account guy. I'm not just a guy who shows up and gives out cards. Let me figure out how we can win business. I'm nothing. Leave me alone, I want to get into this thing, put me in a corner and let me generate new business." Ultimately he agreed.

For the first time I took that responsibility on. I had asked my father to forgo a lot of money; I'd better be ready to step up to the plate. I think I needed the jolt, the super-turbocharged onus on my back of asking my dad, "Pass on this deal." I needed to be backed into a corner in order to get true motivation.

I didn't believe that my dad, in his heart, wanted to sell. I genuinely sensed that he and I could, finally, run this business together. I was twenty-six years old. I may have been the boss's idiot son, but if I could prove myself, I might be able to have an effect.

In 1984 David Deutsch Associates was successful but small and quiet in its profile. We had no more than twenty people in the office and I would prowl around thinking, "How am I going to get some business?" I had a print portfolio with little Oneida silverware ads and soft photo images, and when I'd walk the Eastern Dairy Deli Association trade show and stride into the booths with it, pretty much what I'd hear would be, "Who the fuck is this guy?"

Our president found out from someone at a big agency who had been invited to solicit the account that the Tri-State Pontiac dealers were coming loose. That agency couldn't do it, so out of the goodness of their heart they recommended us.

We would be competing with twenty other agencies. The Pontiac dealers were reviewing Requests for Proposals (RFPs), forms in which agencies basically provide their credentials: billing list, client list, philosophy, work done. The client reviews the RFPs and invites five agencies to pitch the business. On large accounts they may first narrow the list to ten and then go visit the agencies for credentials presentations, kind of a two-hour chemistry check, and then break it down to five. This wasn't a large account, $3 million when our yearly billings were around $10 million, but it was larger than any that we'd ever had.

I looked at our RFP rationally. We had no television experience, we had no car experience; in the natural chain of events the last thing Pontiac was going to do was include David Deutsch Associates on the short list.

How could I make things unnatural? How could I change the playing field? Sometimes the people on the buying side of the equation say, "I have to give these guys a chance." How could I obligate them to talk to me?

The Pontiac Dealers Association included about one hundred dealers in the New York–New Jersey–Connecticut tri-state area. (How many times had I heard that phrase on TV and radio when I was growing up. It was in every local car commercial like a mantra.) They had a guy running the pitch, hiring the agency, managing the process for them, by the name of Bob Conroy. Bob was a gruff, old ex–fighter pilot who had been president of a now-defunct agency, a man who had truly been around the business, a quintessential '50s-'60s ad guy. He had been the lead account man at the agency that had previously won and then lost the Pontiac account, but Pontiac had asked him to advise them where they ought to go next. There was no reason for this guy to put us on the list.

A bunch of us were sitting around trying to figure how to crash this pitch. "Let's do something different," I said. "Outrageous. Out of the box. What can we send him?" Fruit baskets and bottles of booze weren't going to cut it. We brainstormed and finally something clicked. One of my father's partners at the time, a terrific art director named Rocco Campanelli, came up with the idea: used car parts.

We went to a junkyard. Bob lived in Westport, Connecticut, and over the course of a twelve-hour day we delivered a different car part to his house every half hour. One was a headlight, with a tag that read, "We'll give you bright ideas. David Deutsch Associates." Next was a fender—an entire fender of a car showed up in his driveway! "We'll protect your rear end." Then a steering wheel: "We'll steer you in the right direction." By the end of the day he had the entire sedan and a stack of phrases.

It could have backfired. He could have been offended or felt intruded upon or simply pissed off. But Bob was an ad guy; he thought the idea was so clever and so off-the-wall he said, "I've got to go see these guys."

That's what I call the School of Sales Obligation. You do something so creative and so full of extra sweat and thought that the human part of the buyer takes over and he says, "I'm really curious about these guys; at the least they get an hour audience with me."

Bob and I hit it off. He was a guy's guy. I think in many ways he saw me as kind of a son, or a younger version of himself. Of course, he was divorced, a smooth talker and remarried to a much younger woman, so I'm not sure what exactly that means.

Bob really knew his way around the advertising business, and he and I developed an incredibly intimate business relationship. He taught me a lot about client service. He had such a body of knowledge, had been around so long, that I would present him with an idea and he'd say, "Okay, the dealers will say . . ." and he'd know their response before they made it. A wealth of perspective. He would yell at me like a son when I'd fuck up, and I knew he loved me. After my father, I learned more from Bob Conroy than from anyone else in the industry and I owe him a tremendous debt of gratitude. On top of that, he invited us to be one of the five agencies to pitch the business.

In a strange way, because of the charming way we made it to the finals, we went from being no choice at all to almost a favored underdog. Now, did we have a pitch outside the wreck on Bob's driveway? We had four weeks to come up with an idea.

The Pontiac national campaign was "We Build Excitement." The game for the local dealers was, how do they do something that plugs into the national theme but is localized and sells their cars? I came up with one of those so-bad-it's-good ideas. Sometimes advertising has a train wreck linked to it. We developed a ridiculous campaign called "What was the last exciting thing that happened to you?" We sent a film crew out to the corner of Fortieth Street and Broadway in the heart of Manhattan's garment district and asked the man in the street. Fashion Avenue types, teamsters, bicycle messengers, all nationalities, the melting pot. Real people. I could never understand why advertising always showed all these very ad-like characters. Manicured families; handsome, starched businessmen. They didn't look like real people and when they spoke, I didn't believe them for a moment. I believed early on that reality was infinitely more compelling.

We didn't film a commercial; we shot people in the street answering our question: "What was the last exciting thing that happened to you?" This was long before reality TV. We got a lot of "nothing" and "my mother-in-law came over with a rhubarb pie," and the occasional Vinnie Boombatz saying, "My wife left me for an older guy, ha, ha, ha." All with a very New York flavor to it. We strung together a three-minute montage of these boring or stupid but very New York answers and then the announcer came on and said, "Want real excitement? We have a new Pontiac Grand Am for you!" The tag line was "We'll excite you."

The pitch was held in a hotel meeting room. The sixteen head–Pooh-Bah car dealers. This was not an easy crowd. There was a buffet luncheon that the Tri-State executive council indulged in enthusiastically, and each agency paraded in for an hour or two and made their presentation. We screened the montage, showed them storyboards, played it out . . . and they flipped. We got the job!

We were so excited. I was personally exploding when they said, as they awarded us the business, "One of the big reasons we gave it to you is Donny. We want Donny to run the account." That was a watershed moment for me; these guys said they wanted me in there working for them. I wasn't going to argue; it was where I felt I should be.

The account paid us $400,000 a year in fees. That was three or four times the size of our largest client; it grew the agency by maybe forty percent at one pop.

My dad was at the pitch. He was super proud, both for the company and for me. To his credit, he thought, "Okay, wait, I've been running this place for fifteen years and now my idiot son, through his different way of doing things, has landed the kind of account we've never seen before. Maybe this kid's got something. I'm going to let him do his thing a little bit." Though I doubt "do his thing" was in his lexicon. It was more like, "Let's stumble along with Donny for a while."

We won the business in June and had a launch date of November for the new campaign, so over a period of four monthly meetings with the dealers' executive council, we showed them storyboards and talked out the campaign, then went out and shot on the streets for weeks and weeks.

The meetings were always held in a hotel function room. You've got sixteen or eighteen multimillionaires in there, a lot of them self-made or second-generation car guys. Not super-polished but very shrewd businessmen, each with his own opinion, each with a good-size ego. They're looking at the work. They're entrepreneurs, not aesthetes; they're evaluating every ad by thinking, "What's this going to do to my business tomorrow?"

It's a tough room. The advertising industry was becoming increasingly feminized, but cars are one masculine business. It's guy stuff. Car dealers think ad guys are pussies coming in to sell creative work that's going to be cute or flashy but won't be hard-sell. If a car dealer had his way, all commercials would say, *"Buy now! Buy now! Buy now!"* They resist us.

Even if they like a spot, half of them will criticize it just to fuck with you. "Shouldn't there be more car in it?" In other words, "It's not going to drive enough traffic." In fairness to them, dealer ads need urgency and action; they're supposed to create volume in the showroom. But you can't just schlock it up because it's supposed to be something that people want.

We edited six finished commercials and came to the final meeting to present them. The ads would air in three days. We showed the dealers the product. "What was the last exciting thing that happened to you? . . . Pontiac. We'll Excite You!"

Car guys have Pennzoil in their blood; they have great bullshit detectors and they respect strength. I like guys, and these fellas tested me. One dealer, a little old man from New Jersey named Freddy Merkle, raised his hand and said, "What about 'Go Pontiac'?"

"What?"

"You know. 'Go Pontiac!' Let's do a campaign called 'Go Pontiac!' "

"Fred . . ."

The other dealers didn't have my back. They didn't say, "Shut up, Fred, we've already bought this." I swear to God it was almost like sport to them, like I was some kind of gladiator with a sword and shield. Clearly I was in a room with men who would throw the proverbial turd in the punchbowl. They made it very personal. They'd come after you. Like a street fight. A lot of them were bullies and when they kicked sand, you had to kick sand back at them. They leaned away and waited to see if I'd scrap. They wanted to see, "How's this guy going to handle Freddy?"

I said, "Fred, 'Go Pontiac' is interesting and maybe at some point we can introduce it, but, guys, we've been doing this for four months; we have 'What excites you?' now." I kind of danced around and kept on going.

The ads aired. They were a great success. People were talking about them, they got a good buzz, but better than that, the car-buying public in the tri-state area began buying more Pontiacs.

This was the campaign that established, not that Deutsch could do anything, but that on a very visible broadcast stage we could do good work. All of a sudden clients' interests began to be piqued. "We didn't know you could do that. What else you got?" The business began to grow. People want to win.

The "Don't Know Him, Don't Like Him" Syndrome

I'd be more concerned if the people who *did* know me thought I was a schmuck.

It's a constant. Throughout my life I've always had people who don't know me say, from a distance, "I really don't like that guy." I must carry myself in a certain way that people both pay attention to and just don't like. How do I know this? Because sooner or later they meet me and tell me.

I'm not one of those people who live life for what other people think. I want to be liked, I want to be respected, I want to be loved, but I never let it stand in the way of what I want to do or how I want to do it. Fitting in has never been important for me. I always have confidence in my point of view, and when I don't, I fake it as if I own it. That confidence, which breeds success, also breeds a certain amount of animosity. "What gives you the right to think you can do this, should do that?"

I put it out there and I like to back it up. When people smell that, it pisses them off. Many people want to carry themselves with confidence but for their own reasons have trouble pulling it off and end up resenting the fact that they can't live their lives with such certainty. People don't like folks who draw attention to themselves; it seems arrogant; and I understand that it may be threatening to those who aren't so convinced about their own selves. My life has been far from perfect, I've made many mistakes, but I do the Sinatra thing—my way—and people have often found that intimidating. Okay.

Donny Clogs. That's what they called me at the University of Pennsylvania. I wore clogs, those open-back wooden shoes that make you sound like a quarter-horse when you walk down a linoleum corridor or clop across a stone quad on campus. I liked clogs. They were comfortable, they were unusual. There weren't a lot of clogs around. In fact I was breaking new ground. I wasn't trying to say "Fuck you" to anybody, but apparently it pissed off the Top-Siders crowd. Maybe, out of insecurity or shyness or confidence or a combination of the three, I walked with a bit of a swagger. One of my closest friends, Curtis Schenker, who went on to become a super-successful hedge-fund guy, was a year behind me in college. "Here's this guy with a big Jewish afro," he remembers, "who would clump into the commons"—he shuffles like I did (you can't wear clogs without dragging them; half the time they feel like they're falling off your feet)—"put his tray down, go get his drink, and the next thing you know four cute JAPs were sitting around him. Walked around like his shit didn't stink. I said, 'That guy is an asshole but I've got to get to know him.' " Curtis has been my friend for twenty-five years.

On a business level I am personally identified with my company, and Deutsch Inc. is a brand that can be very polarizing. We have always evoked an emotion; that in itself is a good thing. We walk our own path, we don't follow convention, we speak what we feel to be the truth. That outgrowth of arrogance comes at a price: some people don't like us. I take responsibility for that.

Even though we're an organization of one thousand of the

most responsible, dynamic, serious people, my name is on the door and my personality gets associated with everything we do. That has helped win business, but sometimes it has penalized us. Our head of business development will say that often my personal brand and reputation opens doors—"Love to meet you guys. Sounds like Donny's an interesting character." And other times he'll hear, "We don't want anything to do with you guys. We think Donny's an asshole." It cuts both ways, but somehow it's worked for us.

If there are 100,000 people in the advertising industry, there are 98,000 who I don't know, and out of that 98,000 probably 97,000 think I'm a jerk. Why? Because I don't know of their existence. What does that mean? It means somebody somewhere is very jealous of the things I've done. I've made a lot of money, I run an exciting company, I'm the guy TV calls when they want a hot quote or an industry-wide take on a hot topic, and I'm living a dream that they can't live.

No, that's not right; I'm living a dream that *they're not living.*

Big difference.

Why would they like me?—I define their own lack of success.

I'd be more concerned if the people who *did* know me thought I was a schmuck. Then I'd have to consider the idea that maybe I've got a problem. And while I'm sure there are a number of people who think exactly that, I'm glad to say their numbers are considerably smaller than you'd imagine from talking to outsiders. I've done some stupid things over the years. I've made some big-time mistakes, but I've built my success on the idea that a win for me involves a win for everyone around me. I think that counts for something.

The A-to-Z—Culture Concept

Every company has its own set of guiding principles, its own value system. How to unify everyone under one corporate roof.

I don't think anyone ever sets out and says, "Here's how I'm going to build a corporate culture." A culture develops while you live it. If the person who runs a company has a belief system and everything he does stays fairly true to that system, it will attract like-minded people who buy into it, and it then keeps selling itself in concentric circles. As the company grows and accumulates more resources and tools to bring that culture to life, if the value system is firm and entrenched and the company's core group of people are continually selling it outward, that culture gets even more clearly defined.

It starts at the top. My father created David Deutsch Associates. He is a very conservative guy and the shop he founded was refined, elegant, quiet, and print-oriented. The people he hired were men who wore shirts and ties and mirrored his image. When I came on the scene and decided to stay, I found that my dad's and my values were similar and our taste levels were identical—in ten years of working together we never disagreed on an ad—but I couldn't help but notice that we came at things from completely different foundations. I grew up with the tube and my cultural references were popular culture, not classical. Refined? Elegant? Quiet? Print-oriented? I was none of the above. I was aggressive, irreverent, challenging, and funny. My attitude was, "Hey, fuck it, why not?" His was almost the exact opposite.

The way you get attention when you're a small company trying to make a mark is with humor. You can't be considered a creative shop unless you're doing some degree of irreverent work. People equate creative with funny. Look at the infancy of any great agency and you'll find funny ads. Wells Rich Green created Alka-Seltzer's "I can't believe I ate the whole thing." Doyle Dane Bernbach produced the early Volkswagen "Think Small" commercials and the Levy's Rye Bread "You don't have to be Jewish" campaign. Of course, funny ads aren't always successful; the industry is littered with ads that were funny but not effective, and agencies have died as a result. But you've got to get past that.

My father's style was not funny. His work tended to be smart, distinguished, and well-manicured. The game for me was to be irreverent *and* smart.

I hired young guys who saw things my way. It was generational. I was creating an agency-within-an-agency with pop-cultural underpinnings and the desire to laugh out loud. My dad understood what I was doing and never pushed back. He loved it, thought it was great.

I've got to talk about my dad for a moment. I stand on his shoulders every day. He did the hard work; he started the agency from the ground up. I could never have done that. He laid the foundation on which a grand structure was built. My father is more proud of my success than he is of his; he exaggerates my accomplishments and minimizes his own. We are very different characters. The running joke throughout my life: After people meet my father, they ask me, "Where do you come from?" He is the most likable, warm, giving, smart human being you will ever meet. Very true to his values. A class act.

My committing to work with him *at my best* was a wonderful turning point in my life. I had fucked up and he had canned me—how difficult that must have been for a man as serious about his work as my dad. Now I was back and ready to take our business as seriously as he did. After the workday he and I would walk over to the Oyster Bar in Grand Central Terminal, order these delicious, artery-clogging cherrystone pan roasts, and talk about the business, about people. We grew closer, if such a thing was possible.

Growing up, I always felt I had the greatest dad in the world. I loved him more than anything, but we didn't have a father-son bond in which we did tons of activities together; he was always working, providing for his family. We would have catches, we'd go to ball games, I knew he loved me, but we didn't go on fishing trips and such; it just didn't play out that way. He did coach me in Little League one year, which I hated. It was a forced fit; I loved him for doing it, but he didn't belong on the field. My dad was not a sports-jock-nut guy; he was out there to spend time with his son. He had an assistant coach for the nuts and bolts of game instruction, but my father was clearly out of his element and I felt self-conscious and awkward about it. I also sucked at the time; I was a year younger than most of the kids and pretty much everybody was better than I was, which made things even worse.

We did our ultimate guy-guy bonding through this business. He allowed me to bump my head against the wall until I found what worked, and when I did, he could not have been more proud.

I gauged and drove the Pontiac pitch and then many after, and my father began to see a different side of me, one he respected and loved. Sharing the business, both the exhilarations and the anxieties of it—How do we win clients? How do we meet the payroll?—became a source of great love for both of us. He's my biggest fan and supporter, and always has been. A lot of family business stories end badly, this one doesn't. We got to know each other tremendously well as adults; we built a business together; we made each other better; we became best friends.

David Deutsch Associates began doing irreverent work, the kind of work that would get attention, and for the first few years there was a battle for the soul of the agency. In fact, there were two agencies under one roof: one that produced manicured, beautiful, elegant advertising, and another that produced new, irreverent TV work. Two voices were speaking and eventually the new, younger voice emerged as the future voice of the agency. My dad and I would have screaming arguments about three times a year, always over something stupid. But ultimately he was thrilled to work with me, he supported me, and I could not have loved him more. Still do. I've got a great mom who I love very much, and although to this day we argue about how she pushed me as a kid, clearly that's one of the reasons I am so successful. And I was able to create an extra-special bond with my dad by working with him.

In 1988 we created a campaign for Samsung Electronics that featured a young guy lying on his bed in a city apartment, the window open, toying with the TV remote control. He points it at the television, and behind the tube, out the window and across the street, a two-story-high Times Square–type JumboTron billboard changes channels. Interested, the guy walks out on the fire escape, points the remote again, and the *Little Rascals'* Alfalfa pops on the huge screen. He clicks and there's the outsized wrestler Andre the Giant. The sound cuts abruptly just like when you change stations. The guy's surprised; then he realizes that he's in control. The billboard jumps to the Japanese film monster Godzilla. Then Bullwinkle the Moose. As the ad progresses it dawns on the kid that, for that moment, he rules the world. He likes the feeling. "Feel the power," was the tag line. "Samsung Electronics."

The ad made an immediate connection with the brand. These were cultural icons we were jockeying, and to the portion of the TV audience we wanted to lock onto, this ad said, "These guys get it." They liked feeling the power, too. They would buy Samsung.

The actor we used was John Corbett, who a few years later made a name for himself on TV on *Northern Exposure* and then *Sex and the City*.

Once those ads succeeded, the agency began to grow. We won new and big accounts that the agency had never before even approached. The culture of the place began to shift and, to my dad's credit, he saw this was the direction of the future. Not only didn't he stand in its way, he embraced it. Increasingly, he let me run the show.

What's Deutsch Inc.'s shared value system and what type of person plugs into it? The culture of Deutsch, as it has evolved, is all about blazing new trails. About doing things that are leaner, meaner, faster, smarter. We don't want everyone to be the same; we hire all shapes and sizes, men and women, gays and straights, blacks and whites and browns and all colors, middle-aged and younger. We are known around the office—affectionately and with good humor—as "Jews, Chicks, and Fags." We encourage people at Deutsch—we call them "Deutschers"—to be as great as they can be, to be unafraid of failure if it will produce excellence, to go all out. Want to do your best work? Come to Deutsch. Deutschers know this is an A place, so they compete to prove their mettle. They know there are no boundaries; they're not put in a box; they're encouraged to think outside of it. They know advancement is not only possible but right there in front of them. A junior creative can come up with a huge new campaign; it has happened. We don't protect our ass, we're smart and challenging, and we set a high bar.

I try to be all of that. Not that I'm the smartest guy in the world—far from it—but my passion for advertising is contagious. I've driven myself hard these past twenty years because there's been nothing I'd rather be doing, and I am not slow to show my pleasure when other people in our organization succeed. You can be hard on people as long as you're just as hard on yourself. You want someone to show up at the office at five AM? If you're there at four-thirty, they'll be there in a heartbeat. The passion, the competitiveness, the swinging for the fences, it all adds up. If you can bring out the best in people, create an environment in which they do their best work, they will walk through the jungle for you.

If you're the kind of person who keeps a journal, you likely won't work at Deutsch. Dickheads just don't last here politically. Corporate animals don't fit. The rigid stiffen up and leave immediately, if we make the mistake of hiring them in the first place. We're a wonderfully dysfunctional epic family. We have a Deutsch self-portrait: "Big Brains, Big Hearts, Thick Skin, and Two Percent Off-Center." That's a culture worth living in.

The Touch Football Doctrine

Why managing an organization is like choosing up sides.

Successful management in its simplest form is the ability to take a group of human beings and, by understanding their goals and utilizing their individual talents, set up a structure and environment in which you move them to a desired end, your objective.

You can't teach leadership and you can't give power. You can't make people follow you, even if you pay their salary. You have to inspire them. You have to display and embody a vision that will lead the people in your organization to *want* to follow you.

The best bosses understand the people working for them. That's the first component: What makes my people tick? What are they in it for? What's going to move them? Your workers have to know that you understand not only their talents but their need sets, and are respectful of them.

The boss role, manager to manager, the employer role, is a very charged relationship. Think about it. For most people, the only other figures in their lives to whom they have had to be submissive—who, if not telling them specifically what to do, were charged with getting them to be their best and accomplish their greatest goals—were their parents. All that Freudian stuff comes to the table.

It all has to do with each employee's individual makeup and the parents they had. One person might need to be challenged— "Maybe you're not good enough . . ." Another might need attention—"You need my approval . . ." A third might have tremendous confidence and need to hear, "You're smarter than I am and I need your help." Each has to sense that you are aware of him or her as a human being not as simply a means to an end, that you understand their soap opera and will help them toward their goal. They may want career advancement or monetary gain or an emotional/creative outlet; whatever it is, if they know you know it and are working with them to achieve it, they will walk through walls for you.

It's not unlike when I was in high school, choosing up sides for a touch football game in the street.

I was always the organizer. If there were ten guys on the pavement, I was always the one who said, "All right, Perry, you and I'll be captains." My quest was: How do we get a good game out of this? How do we end up with a competitive game where each team has the right balance of super-talented and not-so-talented players, so that everyone is involved, everyone is motivated, and the game doesn't fall apart? I intuitively knew Management 101 at an early age, setting things up so they can succeed.

Being a great manager means being fair. Some self-centered managers have the ability to make people follow them but then set things up purely for their own Machiavellian benefit. So shortsighted. I was never one of those guys who would stack the sides for my team; I wanted a good game, and if it was a blowout, it wouldn't be fun for anybody, the game would end too soon, and we wouldn't play the next day either because nobody'd had a good time.

If we had ten or twelve or fourteen guys out that day, maybe eight or ten or twelve of them were there just to play, to be told what to do. "Zig-out to the Chevy." They wanted to run their routes, catch some passes, and have a good time. Two would be there to control things—me and my friend Perry Schorr. We were more invested, and the games weren't just about the act of the sport. (I don't know whether this means anything, whether aggression breeds success, but of all the guys out there, Perry and I ended up the most financially rewarded. Perry owns a very successful chain of children's clothing stores.)

And here's what management is: Motivating people and putting them in places where they can succeed. You basically want to have a book on everybody; you need to understand who wants to be a leader, who's a follower, who's happy just to be there. Out in the street I had the ability to understand every guy's mental strength, weakness, thought pattern. It came naturally to me. And that's another part of being a good manager: getting inside people's heads.

So here's my book on our game:

LARRY DALE: Great quickness, speedy down the sideline, you
    could hit him with the bomb.
JORY WEITZ: Good speed. Wants to make an impression,
    always goes for the interception.
DAVID GREEN: Slow, but will give extra effort.
PERRY SCHORR: Very competitive, I can get inside his head.
    My best friend.
ME: Terrible hands, will drop everything thrown to him; you
    really don't want this guy at receiver. A field general. Very
    good arm and football sense. Has a game plan. Always the
    quarterback. Knows how to galvanize a team.

So how do you manage these guys? You put David on the line. He'd hand the ball to the opposing quarterback and count, "One Mississippi, two Mississippi." Nothing ever happened at that position and nobody wanted to play it, but that worked for him. David had already achieved his goal; he was out tossing the ball around with Perry and Donny and Jory and Larry.

I'd choose Larry; they'd put Jory on him. Great. I'd say, "Lar, do a double buttonhook, then go long." I knew Jory would bite on the second buttonhook and Larry'd be gone.

Because we were the two quarterbacks, Perry was always on the other team from me. He liked to win and he liked to look good doing it, so he'd always go for the bomb. Queens rules said that three completions was a first down. I know it was kind of un-manly—Real Men Go Deep—but I always knew I could get Perry steamed by chipping him to death with short passes. Six-step down-and-out. Six-step down-and-out. We'd get a couple of cheap first downs. Although Perry was clearly the superior athlete, my play-calling ability got us more touchdowns than we deserved. All the way through junior high and high school we managed to win a lot of games that way.

The Failure-Dichotomy Principle

Failure is good. Failure is not an option. Balance those in your brain.

Creativity is about freedom. In order for people to be free to create, they need to feel free to fail. You can't fear failure. If you want to create a world that values creation above everything else, first and foremost you have to take fear out of the equation. You have to create a culture that can accept failure, live with failure, not be fearful of failure. So much of what we do in life as businesspeople is failure-averse. It's amazing how many businesses and management teams and people I have met make their important decisions based on fear of failure, tripping up, or being ostracized. The driving force for them is not success; it is failure avoidance. No. You need to embrace failure.

Great creative work can't happen without people being willing to look foolish in front of their peers. You need to be free to unload your mind, to have the opportunity to put every idea on the table, no matter how far-fetched or unusual or downright weird. To free up the unconscious while inoculating oneself against ridicule, we have a ritual we call "Shards of Glass." It's a set of words, a preemptive strike against yourself. "This may be a really bad idea, and if it is, throw shards of glass at me . . ." It gives people a safety net so they can sail off into the unknown. "Look, I know this is idiotic, but . . ." At Deutsch I want an entire environment that runs on the principle of "Shards of Glass."

At the same time, you need a culture in which failure is not an option. That seems completely contradictory, but it is possible to have a group of people, an organization, where failure will not be tolerated yet at the same time it can be embraced. I think that's critical in building any brand or organization.

In the process of creating any greatness, breaking any new ground, failure will happen. Yet the mind-set at the same time must be that it can't. If both of those concepts—the ability to fail, yet not tolerating failure—are within the living soul of every person in your organization, greatness will happen. I call that the Failure-Dichotomy Principle.

It's no coincidence that every year in major league baseball the home-run leaders also lead the league in strikeouts. The two go hand in hand. If you're going to swing a big bat, you are going to miss. But it's worth it. Singles hitters make more contact; home-run hitters get the big bucks. Greg Maddux was explaining the facts of baseball life to Tom Glavine in a Nike commercial and said it best: "Chicks dig the long ball."

You can't ever run scared. A team that plays aggressive ball, calls the hit-and-run a lot, will sometimes run itself out of a rally or hit into a double play. In an environment that's built on winning, that may sound contradictory. More often than not, however, they'll score. If you are running scared of losing a piece of business, running scared of not winning an account, running scared of doing an ad that is critiqued negatively, you will lose them all. In a successful creative workplace there needs to be something in the air, in the walls, in the people, *in the DNA,* that understands that it's okay to swing for the fences and strike out, even if you miss terribly.

I ought to know.

When we are considering ideas, I always look at the handle boards. Now, *storyboards* present the details of an ad—words, music, graphics—combined for ease of presentation onto a series of Fome-Cor illustration boards. My belief is that a great idea can always be culled down to one sentence with a paragraph describing it, which we put on a single board I can get a handle on. A handle board. If I can't tell you my idea in a sentence and go "Here it is," it's not a great idea. If I need pictures, if I need descriptions of shots—no good.

We were pitching Domino's Pizza. Domino's had a quality issue. People didn't believe, because it arrived so quickly, that it could be any good. So the problem we had to solve was, How do we up the quality issue?

My staff presented me with a bunch of ideas. On one of them, even as one of my partners and favorite people, our creative director Kathy Delaney made the presentation with all the creatives in the room, she said, "I know we can't do this, but every time they present it to me, I can't kill it because I just laugh every time." The line was, "Domino's—Bad monkey, good pizza."

The idea was we would create a character—a monkey, a real monkey that's very mischievous, a Curious George–like critter— that is always doing everything in his power to keep Domino's from making great pizza. A foil. He keeps messing with them and they keep hanging in there, and no matter how off-the-wall he gets, they still turn out great pies. "Domino's. Bad monkey, good pizza."

Any sane person looks at that idea and says, "You can't do that! It's a monkey. How can you put a monkey in a food place? It's unsanitary and it's ridiculous. You just can't do it. They're gonna laugh at us." Domino's was a big account, a real midwestern company; we were a long shot. We just said, why not? What's the worst that could happen? The client laughs at us, the client throws us out of the room. It was one of those ideas. You show up, put a smile on your face. Go for it.

We presented that idea along with two others to the client. They fell in love with it. The clients thought it was great, outrageous, wonderful. That sounded to us like a lesson—don't be afraid of failure. There was a win.

Well, here comes the loss.

First off, we couldn't use a real monkey. The client said the little pieces of sausage on the pizza were going to look like monkey droppings. Can't risk that. Got to use an animated monkey or a fleece. Something that didn't shit.

Domino's had an African-American agency that was going to translate the work into the urban community. They took one look at the monkey and found it racist, a stereotype, a black monkey. I thought that was ridiculous. We weren't talking about color; we were talking about a simian! I thought it was racist of them to look at this disarming little critter and inflict the issue of race on it. *It was a monkey! An animal!*

The client got all nervous. They ran some focus groups and one out of every ten or fifteen people said, "Yeah, maybe it is." Can't have that because, unfortunately, if ten people write in and complain that Domino's is running racist advertising, and Al Sharpton gets a hold of it, Domino's could find itself in a disastrous hole. Like it or not, we were screwed.

But they still liked the idea of a critter, so we changed him a little. Instead of a monkey we created a Tasmanian Devil–type Muppet-looking character, a weird little thing we called Bad Andy. "Bad Andy, good pizza."

We made the commercials and they missed. They were awful. The character wasn't funny, it wasn't warm, it was just weird. People saw it and thought, What is that weird little thing doing here? The franchisees saw it and hated it, business was terrible, it was a disaster, and eventually we lost the business.

We swung and we missed. You have to be able to accept the fact that any time you do something different, you're setting yourself up for people to find you wanting. We tried an untraditional pizza-selling concept and it didn't work. But for every miss like that we have the Ikeas, the Mitsubishis, the Tylenols, the Expedias. It happens and you have to be able to accept it, laugh at it, and get back to work. If you are not willing to have a Bad Andy, if you are not willing to embrace failure, then you are not willing to have a place with creativity in the walls.

Sometimes failure doesn't allow you to embrace it. Sometimes it just envelops you.

When David Deutsch Associates hit 1989, 1990, we started to go to the next level. Our client base was expanding; our creative output was getting highly noticed; we were starting to make some money. My dad was pretty much retired at that point and I was seen in the industry as a renegade crazy guy with big hair, hardly the right person to head a substantive agency. *Adweek* began a company profile with "Donny Deutsch is impossible. Just ask anyone— even him." I felt we needed a legitimate business person to serve as our second face to the industry, so I went out, did a search, and in September, 1991, ended up hiring a guy named Steve Dworin. We took him away from J. Walter Thompson, where he was executive vice president and head of account management. Steve was a well-regarded man with standing in the community. A real suit.

As a general rule, I would rather have fifty-one percent of something huge than one hundred percent of a small bundle. As part of his compensation package I gave Dworin ten percent of the agency. My thinking was, number one, that's the only way you get really talented people to come to a small place, and number two, if someone feels like they own a piece of the shop, they are going to go out of their way to grow it into a major success. Sounded reasonable. So when Dworin asked for it, I gave him ten percent of the business for pretty much nothing. In addition, after two years he was to receive another ten percent. He would end up a twenty percent owner. It was a tool that I used to bring him on board. I thought I had cut a good deal.

I had absolutely no idea that this ran completely contrary to small-business conventional wisdom. I had a discussion with a friend about hiring in his own industry and suggested, "Why don't you give away . . . ?"

"Give away?!" He looked at me like I was crazy. It was the small-family-business mentality: *Never give away equity.* But I never cared much for conventional wisdom.

Hiring Steve was a smart move for a couple of reasons. He was intelligent, he definitely helped expand the business, and he gave us the appearance of propriety. *The New York Times* ran an article announcing the hiring, and even the photo of us together— me with my big hair, him in his suit—said everything we wanted it to.

Yet, there was something in my gut when I hired him; I didn't know how *good* of a guy he was. Steve was very bright but mercurial. When I'd started at Ogilvy & Mather, he had been three or four levels above me, and I remembered him as a hard-charging character, kind of difficult but obviously a talented, successful guy.

For the first year things went great. We won the LensCrafters account, we won Tanqueray, we won Prudential Securities. We worked the '92 election for Bill Clinton. We went from annual billings of $90 million to $250 million in two years. Then things started to get a little strange. Before the year was out Dworin, who was hired for his conservative attire, started to dress like me. At the time I was in the habit of wearing loud sport jackets, T-shirts, and cowboy boots, and he began to wear the same outfits.

I had begun to get a lot of media attention and that seemed to bother him. A magazine called *Creativity* called to profile me; at the time, I was creative director. When he found out there was going to be a story, Steve said "Why is it just you on the cover?" Duh. *Creative* director? *Creativity?* But because I wanted peace in the office, and because I was afraid of losing him, I called and begged the magazine to include him. Steve was the company president; he didn't belong in the article. I supported him. When CNN's *Pinnacle* wanted to run a story on me, he was upset enough that I begged the producer, "Can you do it on both of us?" They included him.

We pitched Hardee's fast food and got the gig. Dworin's mother had been sick, or something of the sort, and he hadn't been able to get to one of the pitches. When we got the job, it seemed to me the guy was actually bummed out. This was a big win for us at the time, but he didn't seem happy for us; if he wasn't there, if he wasn't part of the process, it wasn't a win for him.

But I was not smart enough or strong enough to do anything about it. I should have said, "Look, motherfucker, this is it: Number one, you're out of line; number two, you are always going to be number two here. It is what it is and it is a huge opportunity for you." Instead, I tried to put us on even footing. After a year and a half, when he was president and doing well, he came to me and said, "People don't even know I'm a partner here, they think because my name's not on the door that I'm just an employee." I was such a moron that I actually kowtowed to him; we changed the agency's name from David Deutsch Associates to Deutsch/Dworin. Why? Because I was stupid and I was afraid of losing him. We had a successful formula, the suit and the wild man, and I felt the combination was so good I didn't want to mess with it.

With the name change, his profile began to rise. We were making money, this wild man he was stuck with and him, the responsible citizen. I owned eighty percent yet my title was executive vice president/creative director; he owned twenty percent and he was president of the agency now named Deutsch/Dworin. I didn't care that my title was EVP because I knew I owned the large majority of our stock, but it was certainly the wrong signal to send. Not only could people in the industry be excused if they perceived us as on the same level, but it would not have surprised me if they thought the credit had shifted as well.

The climate of the agency had begun to change. I had always tried to make the Deutsch workplace feel like home, a place you wanted to stay all night long and then some. Now the office started to cloud up. I liked open discussions; Dworin seemed to favor something different. He would take executives aside and whisper in their ears. The boss tells you something, you're likely to listen.

Very early on Dworin approached Linda Sawyer—who had been at the agency for three years, was one of my closest confidantes, and at that point, was account director on Ikea, one of our most important accounts—and took his best shot. See if she'd bite. She didn't.

Dworin and I began increasingly not to see eye to eye. At one point he quit and I talked him out of it. "Okay, Steve, what do you want?" I wasn't taking him on. I was, in fact, letting him take more and more control of the clients. Because he was the account guy, the person whose responsibility it is to make sure the clients are soothed and happy, Dworin was the front man, the first point of contact between us and the people who ran the companies who paid us. All the clients thought he was the smartest man in the world; that's what I'd hear. Look at the work we were delivering them, look at our results! Who was responsible? The man who said he was responsible, the man who had their ear. And in his own way, I sensed, Steve was trying to take control of the agency, because— and this is Advertising 101—if you own the clients, you own the agency. It was my own fault; I didn't know what I wanted. Was I a creative? Was I a businessman? What the fuck was I?

This kind of anxiety wasn't normal for me, but at that time my life wasn't in the least bit normal. I was in the middle of a rocky relationship with my wife; we kept separating. I was living out of a suitcase in one of those month-to-month residential hotels. I was in and out of relationships, dating other women, drinking, partying more than was healthy. Gaining weight. I wasn't sleeping. I'd go to bed at eleven, wake up at quarter to twelve, and be up all night. So I was operating on zero sleep, under tremendous stress at work, had to function, couldn't function. I was seeing a therapist who wouldn't prescribe medication to help me sleep even though I was clearly in shambles. It was a bad time for me. I looked at the business, saw that it was going well, said, "Okay, this guy is running the ship," at least felt secure in that area while the rest of my life was crashing around me, and pulled back a bit.

Because he was ten percent owner, Dworin was supposed to receive ten percent of the first year's profits; but when I went to give it to him, he told me, "I've done so much more than you expected; I do as much as you do and I should get more than just the ten." If an executive comes to Ford Motors, does some good, and then tells them, "I'm working as hard as you are; we should be splitting the earnings," would Chairman and CEO Bill Ford disregard the fifteen years that came before, ignore the basic precepts of capitalism and roll over for him? I don't think so. But I was weak, I was stupid, I gave Dworin twenty-five percent of the first year's profits.

It wasn't enough. If I didn't stop it, the agency would eventually be called Dworin. But I was a schmuck. I made two horrendous mistakes: I didn't listen to my gut when I initially considered hiring him (your gut always tells you about people; you don't always want to listen, but the information is always in there) and I was too weak to take him on. Dworin, meanwhile, was flashing his strength.

Steve had brought in a lot of his own people, which is what executives do when they gain authority in organizations, pack them with acolytes. Among his hires was a man named John Tracosis, a really solid citizen. He had been at Ogilvy when I'd been there. A big ex-Cornell football player. Tracosis was having problems with a client, he was not performing well, so Steve and I took him out for dinner to see if we could fix it. We weren't to the point where we were putting him on probation, just kind of a "Hey, John, you've really got to take it to the next level. It's not working, here's why." People have these dinners all the time.

Technically, because John was an account guy and Steve was head of the account guys, John worked for Steve. Steve went to work on him. He told Tracosis that the clients didn't think John was very bright, that he didn't think Tracosis had it anymore, that the job was passing him by. The goal may have been to shock an employee into improving his performance but I didn't like the way Dworin did it.

Steve played such a bad cop that I had to chime in as the good one. I could not just sit there. I did my best to let Tracosis know that we were with him and "we'd get it right."

I was not pleased with the way Dworin had handled the situation. This was not the atmosphere I wanted in my company. The next morning I had breakfast with Linda Sawyer and said, "What do you think would happen if I got rid of Steve?"

I was very surprised when she told me, "People would be happy."

I hadn't realized that even the people he'd brought in were halfway out the door. I'd known there were some morale problems, but I'd said to myself, "Okay, it's better for business; maybe this is what it has to be." We were on a roll, we were winning clients and making money.

I had lost my way. I was not smart enough to know that we could take the next step and grow the business without turning into the stereotypical unhappy place to work. I guess the reason I hadn't heard about any problems was that people thought he and I were so tight they were afraid to come to me. I wasn't clearheaded enough to feel the silence. It was my responsibility and I had failed to realize it. Linda cleared that up in a flash.

"Donny, it would be a good thing. I don't care even if we go backward in business; we'll go forward."

But I couldn't can him; I figured the clients would follow him out the door.

We were on a plane coming back from a client meeting a few days later when I turned to him and said, "You know what, Steve, I'm going to make myself CEO."

"I don't know why you'd do that," he said. "You're not a title guy; what do you need that title for?"

"I feel comfortable doing it," I told him. "It's the title I want."

"The CEO is usually the business guy. Why don't you make yourself chairman?"

"No, I'm fine with CEO."

As the flight progressed Steve kept standing up and walking to the back of the plane. These were the days when there weren't phones on the back of each seat. There were only a limited number of telephones onboard. I think he was going back there making calls.

This was February 1994. A big snowstorm hit New York the next day. I made my way to work and his office was pretty much cleaned out. Not one hundred percent, but clearly someone had come in and removed a lot of stuff. He walked into my office with his chest all stuck out and, as I recall, said, "I've been thinking a lot about it and you making yourself CEO, this is bullshit. I'm carrying all the load around here and you are talking about making yourself CEO. I'm on my way out. This is not working for me." He looked at me. I don't know what he saw. "I've pretty much made up my mind to leave, but I've got a few more things to do. I'm going down to my office and I'll be back in about fifteen, twenty minutes and you tell me what you come up with. Maybe you'll have a different offer for me. Maybe you can up the equity stake. Maybe you want to think again if you want to make yourself CEO."

Pure power play.

I had put his name on the door; now he was taking his toys and going home. As muddled as I might have been, it was clear to me that we could no longer work together. I made up my mind that that was it.

Twenty minutes later Dworin strode back in, his chest puffed out as if he'd been pumping iron. He slid open the glass doors of my office, expecting capitulation. I held up my hand and moved my fingers up and down, as if to say, "See ya."

In cartoons, color drains from a character's face until it's white-white. Dworin blanched. He tried to speak but his mouth was cotton. I'd never seen such a physical transformation before; it was as if he'd been seared.

"Well, maybe we can talk." He sounded like he couldn't get any saliva. "I want you to think about it." He walked back to his office.

I went to another floor of our offices so he wouldn't be able to find me. "Let me know when he's gone," I told my assistant. I didn't want him coming back crying and trying to make up. I wanted this thing over.

But he didn't come back. He'd overplayed his hand and had been called. He had no choice but to do what he said he was going to do and resign.

Dworin cleared out his office, this time for good.

Steve was gone, but we had a big problem now. We didn't want the press to find out. We were an agency that was kicking ass, winning client after client with great work. But once word got out, *Advertising Age, Adweek, The New York Times, The Wall Street Journal,* and the entire advertising press community would call Steve and ask, "Why did you leave? You guys were on this great roll. What did

Donny do to you that you left? Was he stealing money? Were there drugs involved? Was he abusive?" And Steve, this legitimate businessman, so pedigreed, could say anything. Must be crazy Donny. Steve was in the catbird seat, and we were very vulnerable. He was the major liaison with several of our most important clients; he was in direct contact; one word from him and our major sources of income could start walking out the door *on his arm*. He could take them with him! Dworin had a noncompete clause in his contract, but those clauses are very difficult to enforce. And more to the point, you can't keep clients from doing what they want to do; if they don't want you, you can't keep them. The agency could crumble.

What held us together was that Steve didn't want any word out on the street yet either; we hadn't worked out a severance package. Steve wanted money. Technically, even though he owned twenty percent of the company, because of the kind of stock he owned and because he had walked out on us, he was not guaranteed a penny. Our position was, "Screw you, you quit. That's it. Later for you, you don't get something for quitting." Nobody knew how this was going to play out.

A day went by. It was a snowy Friday. By late afternoon I'd heard nothing from Dworin. I walked into Linda Sawyer's office. Linda is a wonderful human being. She had been with me for years. Focused, caring, incredibly smart, she was the person to whom I could tell everything.

I slumped down in a chair and started crying. I'd never done that before, certainly not in the office. Exhausted, frightened, drained, seeing everything I'd worked to create coming apart in the face of my own timidity, stupidity, irresponsibility. I told her everything and Linda, to her everlasting credit, talked me through it.

I can't say enough good things about Linda Sawyer. She arrived at the agency in 1989 and has been my right hand all these years. She is the yin to my yang. Other than my father, there is no one more responsible for the agency's success than she. Linda is my alter ego at the office and my heir apparent.

Late Saturday, Dworin called. "I think we should meet for breakfast tomorrow and talk things over." That was fine with me.

We started out very civilly over our eggs. "It's too bad it worked out this way"—that kind of bland, mealymouthed introduction. Then Steve said, "You know, I want this to work out. I hope you're going to do the right thing by me, because what happens if we have to get lawyers involved? Then we have to start talking about business and I've got to start talking about what a crazy business environment it was." He mentioned several of the wilder moments in my on-the-job history.

"You motherfucker!" That was it for me. "You want to go there, I'll go right there with you!" He paused. I knew at that moment that if I said, "Fuck you, I'm going to a lawyer, kiss my ass," my business could have blown up. I held my tongue. "So," I said, "are we going to do this like fucking businessmen?"

Our lawyers did get involved—and very quickly—but only to negotiate a settlement. That went as well as could be expected. In a typical situation of this kind between a company and a departing executive, the company is concerned about losing clients and the executive is concerned about money. This worked out in a typical way. Six years later I sold the company for close to $300 million. What I ended up paying Dworin was insignificant in comparison.

The ad press, as expected, jumped all over the story. Is Deutsch going to fall apart? What did Donny do? Crazy Donny. Was Donny not capable of sharing the limelight? Did Donny's ego take over? Little did they know that I wasn't the ego-driven maniac in this particular fight; I just played one on TV.

(Splitting up made Dworin *the* name of the moment in advertising. For two months in the ad trades the big question was, "Where's Steve going?" Drove me nuts. He had arrived as the classic suit, but he was really wearing the emperor's new clothes. He landed a job as chairman and CEO of the venerable N.W. Ayer & Partners, a much larger agency than ours that had been hit by hard times. Big job for him, big articles in the trades. From there he went to Tatham in Chicago, running all of Procter & Gamble's advertising. Took a couple of years and he was gone from there, too. I've barely run into him since.)

I gathered everyone in the office. "Look," I said, "Steve is leaving."

The place filled with a happy buzz. Linda knew what she was talking about.

There was so much to be done. The business was extremely vulnerable. With Steve gone clients could think, "Maybe it's not the same agency anymore." We had the potential to unravel. I had the potential to unravel. We had to combat that.

I jumped on the phone with clients. I couldn't afford not to. LensCrafters had been Steve's client; now it was mine. Its senior vice president and director of marketing was Dave Richards. "Dave," I said, "tell me what's a win for you. Tell me what needs to happen for you in the next year, what is going to show you that this is the agency you need. I need to work back from that." He told me, "We're not going to leave the agency tomorrow, but you are on notice." I could accept that. Clients weren't abandoning ship.

I dug in. The entire company went to work, but it wasn't easy. We had to make Steve's major clients—Prudential Securities, LensCrafters, and Tanqueray—see that the creative product was what the agency was all about and stay onboard.

We stayed steady, which was a home run. We didn't lose any clients, which was critical. Business as usual was a big win.

I, personally, was up against the wall. For years my father had been the grown-up in the organization and I was free to be crazy Donny creating a new persona for the agency, elevating the creative product. Then Steve had taken on the grown-up's role, doing all the compensation deals and frontline client work. Now there was no one in the organization to take overall responsibility except me. I had to grow up as a businessman; I couldn't be a crazy creative guy anymore.

And I did. I started dressing differently; all of a sudden I was in a suit. I did things I'd never done at the agency. I became the main account guy, the frontline liaison with clients. I started to get involved in and sign off on strategic documents, set up credit lines, decide who was getting what bonus in all areas of the company. I began dealing with the banks, dealing with lawyers, dealing with every financial piece of the business. When I looked into the mechanics of being a businessman, I found it wasn't rocket science. My father did it. Steve did it. There was an industry-wide formula for some of these things, and when I looked at it closely, I started to realize that the work my father and Steve had been doing wasn't as difficult as I had assumed. Things that had been mysteries all of a sudden became clear.

Compensation agreements, for example. A compensation deal lays out the financial underpinnings of how much we get paid, and I had never created one. The way agencies are paid for the most part is on the basis of time of staff. The client gives us the scope of work involved: "For the next year we are going to do this media plan; we need this kind of advertising, direct mail, this and that." We come back and say, "Here's the staffing that you need on the business side: You need seventeen account people: seven senior and ten junior. You need twenty-one media people: twelve associate media directors, six media directors, three juniors. You need twenty-four creative people: eight creative teams. You need eighteen research people . . ." We put the entire staff in place. These people have direct salary costs, so there is a total yearly salary number which is X. We include our overhead, which is a computation of everything else including rent, supplies, and so on. Then you add twenty percent profit and that is the compensation package. You tell the client it comes to, let's say, $14.4 million per year, and that's how we get paid. Not that complicated. I even found it interesting.

My domain had been the creative group. Now it was everything. I had to be *The Guy*. The guy who signed off on media plans; the guy who balanced the financial concerns of the agency with the creative concerns of the people who turned out the work; the guy who had to take every client's president out to dinner—in a suit.

When I met with those presidents, I found that the same people skills I used in the creative department worked just fine for me there as well. I liked it. I liked being more than just the ad guy. In fact, I actually liked it more.

I grew up. I made myself CEO and I had to start acting like a CEO. It was a tremendous time of growth for me. I was thirty-five years old and for the first time I didn't have a safety net. I had been a creative leader but I'd never been a real executive before, and I found I was a good one.

Very often, you grow the most from handling your biggest failures in your hardest times. I certainly did. From the most painful business experience I'd ever had, I learned how to manage, I learned what kind of people I wanted to hire. Certain failures, even if they're painful, even if they seem to be half-steps backward at the time, can propel you twenty steps forward. Deutsch Inc. weathered failure and I personally embraced it.

At the same time that you acknowledge and embrace failure, there are moments in business and in life when you have to say, "Failure is not an option." We as human beings have a mirror in which we see ourselves and say, "Okay, what have I got?" At some point you put your own back to the wall.

Certain battles are more crucial than others. For instance,

when a man falls so madly in love with a woman that he knows he can't be in love with anyone else, he says, "This woman is the love of my life. I can't let this woman get away." At that point he tells himself, "Failure is not an option." Championship NBA teams play eighty-two regular-season basketball games a year; they don't look themselves in the mirror every night and say, "We will not lose." They can't. You can't do it that way. It doesn't mean they aren't giving their best every night. When the playoffs come around and they're playing for the championship, that's when they make their stand.

We all, as human beings, have a depth gauge within ourselves and at some point we decide that the game, the championship, the job, our soul, is on the line. At that point you simply can't allow yourself to fail.

There are agencies who are good losers, places where losing is not only accepted, it becomes part of the culture, it is expected. That is debilitating. Don't let that happen to you. At Deutsch we go into every pitch assuming we are the Yankees. It's amazing what happens when you go into a room full of smart, hungry people and say, "Failure is not an option." People are galvanized.

When I was young and my dad was still running the business, we had the opportunity to go up against some of the first-tier agencies on a pitch for Ikea. Chiat/Day was top dog, a much bigger, much more prominent agency than we were, and they were odds-on favorites. I had hired a bunch of young, crazy rebels and I told them, "Guys, this is where we're going to prove we're better than everyone else." I hit the hot button; I knew, because it was a key reason I had hired them, that each one of these guys had something to prove. They hadn't gotten their due; they were a little pissed off that the people ahead of them—no more talented, no better than they were—were getting all the glory.

"Who's better?" I said. "You or Chiat/Day? It's really fucking simple as that. Now's the time to prove it. This is a highly regarded account; we're in the door, we have an equal shot. Who's better, them or us?" If we'd been in a huddle on a field in front of fifty thousand fans, we'd have been screaming. "This is where you make your bones. You're going to do your first great TV campaign. Just playing the game is not good enough here. A good try is not good enough here. This is our time, this is our place. It might take a lot of years to get back here, we may not get another shot at this at all, and we're not going to blow it. We have the tools to win; we're up against the best guys in the industry. We cannot *not* succeed. Failure is not an option on this one."

We took that baby home.

Zig Theory

Don't play in someone else's universe; define your own.

Many people wake up every morning and say, "I know what I am going to do today. I've got a job; I've got a boss; I've got things to do; there are rules and I go by them. That's the way it's always been done; that's what I'm going to do."

There is another way. There are many other ways.

In the advertising industry there are "creative" awards given annually to creative teams at ad agencies for individual pieces of work, so many awards I can't even count. They're basically knocking out awards for everything. Best television, best radio, best print, best outdoor, best business-to-business. There are awards for best pharmaceutical advertising, best financial advertising . . . You've got the CLIOs, the One Show, Cannes, the Beldings in Los Angeles; you've got local award shows. These awards are announced at gala award shows where each year everyone gets dressed up, agencies buy tables, and the entire advertising world competes to see who's the big cheese for the next twelve months. All of these award shows publish award books, compilations of the award-winning work. Young creatives travel with these award books to show colleagues and prospective employers exactly what kind of award-winning people they are and what kind of award-winning work they produce. It's stunningly self-congratulatory.

I routinely walk around our office. (I've always managed by walking around. Any CEO or leader who spends the majority of his time in his office is not doing his job.) One morning I passed two young creatives sitting around drinking coffee, thumbing through the books. I had seen them do this before.

"What are you guys doing?" I asked. They didn't appear to be hard at work.

"Well, you know," one of them said to me, "we're just trying to get ideas, trying to get stimulated." Obviously they had done this often. He was explaining their pregame ritual. "We like to look at great work."

I went nuts on them.

"Do you see how fundamentally flawed that is?" They looked at me with open faces. They didn't.

"Well"—the young guy speaking clearly felt peculiar, first because the boss was mad at him and he didn't know why, and second because he thought he was explaining the obvious—"this is the kind of stuff that wins awards."

He was missing the point entirely. "Yeah, so?" I was losing the battle to keep my voice down. "You're looking at what award-winning work looks like, so already you're going to try and play in that box. At *best* you are going to come out with a warmed-over version of something that has already been done.

"Start a blank page. That's not saying that work's not good, and obviously you should take it all in, but if that's what you're using for creative stimulation, you're already training your mind to work in a simple universe. You're playing in somebody else's universe. Define your own!"

On TV news, where did it get written that an anchorwoman has to have anchorwoman-looking hair? You know the look—dated, helmet-like—you've seen it for decades. Producers and on-air stylists automatically think—without considering that maybe there is a better way, in this case a better hairdo—"Oh, that's what an anchorwoman looks like." This kind of unquestioning devotion to sameness pervades our society. It pervades what an office is supposed to look like, how people are supposed to dress, what makes a good ad.

Of course, you're not going to break new ground if you don't have confidence. Confidence. Not necessarily that you have all the answers, but that at least you are entitled to go your own way. *Things don't have to be done the way they've always been done.* Any pioneer is going to know this instinctively. It's not arrogance; it's natural thought process. The biggest winners in the world are the people who somehow, right or wrong, are able to use their own universe as a grading system. They don't need anybody else's boundaries; they don't play in anybody else's sandbox.

In fact, our society, given the opportunity to choose, loves "different." Creative presentations, for example. Early in my years as head of the agency we would often show our ideas to clients handwritten on flip charts, because it just seemed smarter and easier and more raw than the conventional slick presentation that they had been seeing for decades. It also made a statement about who we were: refreshingly simple and all about the ideas. At Deutsch we never do something different for its own sake; we're different with a purpose.

Whenever someone starts giving me client intelligence and says, "We hear Joe likes big productions" or "We can't do demonstrations because the client doesn't like that," I always tell them, "Do what is right for the business. Just make the god *What Is Going to Move the Product in the Marketplace.* Pitching a client is the only time you have the complete freedom of a consultant; you don't have to worry about individual agendas, just go in and do what is right." That tends to work out. It seems very obvious, and you can't be an idiot about it; you should use as much knowledge as you have about your audience. But at the end of the day, your opening pitch is the one time you have the luxury of objectivity.

Several years ago the pharmaceutical industry was at the bottom of the advertising food chain. It was seen throughout the field as a low-rent, uninspired, very constricted product group. No creative agency the likes of Chiat/Day or Fallon or Goodby would go near those things. It wasn't sexy. It was medical advertising; you couldn't do good work. At that time Pfizer came to us and wanted us to pitch an allergy drug, Zyrtec. All the larger multi-national agencies were invited to pitch, and some bit, including J. Walter Thompson, McCann-Erickson, Ogilvy. But they all went in grumbling.

Everyone was saying it wasn't a creative account. I took a different approach. I said, "Wait a second, why can't it be a creative account?" Number one, just because nobody had done good pharmaceutical work in the past twenty years didn't mean we couldn't be the first. Number two, you are talking about somebody's health, someone's well-being. To me, that work should be a lot more creative and emotional than work for, say, a car or a soft drink. Which is more important? Why did it get written that sneaker advertising can be good creatively, and beer advertising can be good creatively, but when it comes to someone's well-being, creativity is out of the question? I didn't understand that at all. Number three, Pfizer was investing a lot of money and I realized, boy, if somebody ever could crack it and do fresh work, the floodgates would open. Why? As we baby boomers start to age, this was exactly where big advertising would be going.

It wasn't brain surgery, but somehow we were the only ones who figured it out.

Sometimes you don't have to be out of the box; sometimes you simply need to find the top of the box and work right there. Maybe it won't be as breakthrough as something you might do for a younger product like Snapple, but if you do it smart and well, your work will shine in comparison to what has been done before.

One of our competitors, a well-regarded creative agency, dropped out of the pitch because they were getting pressure from inside their shop that it couldn't be done. Even my own people were lacking in enthusiasm. "It's pharmaceuticals," my creatives told me. "You don't want to pitch that shit."

"Guys," I said, "trust me. I'm not telling you to do crappy work. Yes, there will have to be fifteen seconds of 'fair balance,' where you need to include all the boring but necessary fine-print information, because that's legal. Other than that, forget what the product is and go for good work."

Zyrtec is a medication that controls many kinds of allergies, from pollen to dust to pet dander and much more. We researched the product, looking for clues to connect it to its customers in a compelling way. We found that the vast majority of allergy sufferers had a personal relationship with their allergies. I don't want to say these folks took pride in their symptoms, but they *wore* them; the ailment became part of their personalities. They'd tell us with a mixture of distress and possession, "I'm allergic to pets and feathers," "I'm allergic to green grass," "I'm allergic to cotton." One of our partners and chief strategy officer, Cheryl Greene, came up with the breakthrough insight: Their health was affected so deeply that their allergies almost defined them. Cheryl is one of the most brilliant people I have ever worked with. She is Deutsch Inc.'s central brain and nervous system, one of the key people responsible for the growth of the agency.

We came up with a series of television commercials, shot in black-and-white, in which average-looking people look you in the eye and define themselves. A young boy standing next to his brother says, "I'm a cat-pollen-dust-mite." His mother tell us, "And Billy's a mold-ragweed-cat."

"I'm three!" the little brother exclaims.

Nice and simple. We turned their afflictions into badges of honor that, instead of being an embarrassment, became part of their wardrobe. On a more fundamental level, what we did was recognize people's individuality and celebrate it.

We won the business. The ads were knockouts, and they won us more pharmaceutical clients, which then won us even more. And guess what: All the other good creative agencies realized, "Wow, you can do good work here! This is a growing business. We can do pharmaceutical advertising and still think of ourselves as cutting-edge."

Now, what had we done? We had looked at the future as full of possibility and then stepped in and fulfilled it.

People always tend to look at what *is* today and then stop. It is amazing how often business decisions are based on what *is* rather than what *can be*. Who decided where and when you can do creative advertising? Who pasted on that label?

Our growth in the pharmaceuticals category was staggering. Zyrtec alone was a $100 million account. Yet if a $2 million imported-beer client came up for grabs, everybody would be chasing after it. I don't see why. Frankly, it is more fun to do creative work where it has never been done before.

You have to have your own litmus test. So many people enter so many moments in life with a mind-set predicated on a playing field or a paradigm or a rule set or value system just because it exists. In pitching the agency to clients, I often say, "In the advertising business, so many things are done because that's the way they've always been done. We don't do that."

In the typical creative exploratory, clients give agencies four weeks to two months to come back with work. It's an extended period of time. Why? Instead of six weeks, give people six days; you'll save five weeks and a day and you'll actually get better work because the teams are forced into linear thinking. Creative minds feel obligated by nature to go all over the place for answers. But when there's an urgency attached, brains are forced to work in overdrive.

I say to clients when I'm pitching them, "We've tried to build a business the way it should be, not the way it *is* set up. Why do creative exploratories have to take six weeks? Why does the average commercial have to cost $400,000? Because that's what it's supposed to cost? If you give creative people $40,000, they're certainly not going to waste money on production values, so they'd better come up with an idea, because that's all they've got!" Clients love to hear this, because what we are saying is, "You are not stuck in convention."

Why is the account director the first point of contact with a client? I don't know anymore. I don't know if that funnel still works. You have to have a knowledge base—you can't barge in like an idiot, you have to be informed—but any number of people in an organization could talk to a client without the foundation of the industry collapsing. Maybe if you were starting from scratch, you wouldn't have a function called "account management." You might have a two-person contact, a creative and an account person who always talk to the client together, a "brand duo." But things have just been done a certain way and so people keep right on doing them.

The real winners are the ones who ask, "How should this be done? How would I do it if there were no conventions, if there were no predispositions?" And you know, that's it! When they show up with the answers, that's when greatness comes.

It's hard to get to. Many people approach new fields by thinking, "I'm smart enough to learn how it's done and then do it that way." The first time an incoming creative gets an advertising assignment, he or she tries so hard to write an "ad." That way lies mediocrity. Don't write an ad, write something that moves me.

We run focus groups all the time to help gauge the success of our work, rooms full of ordinary people with no connection to the ad industry and only a basic connection to the product field. Often we get stung. If we ask the people sitting around that table to screen several choices and tell us which one they like best, they almost invariably play back the ads that look like what an ad "should" look like. They think this makes them look smart.

But that is what's wrong with everything! Forget ad experts; the people in that room don't have enough confidence to say what they like, as opposed to what they've been taught to like. It takes courage to embrace something that looks dramatically different, and they don't want to seem stupid to their peers.

This is why the traditional focus-group method almost ensures that we get very like-minded responses. We'll show people new ads and they'll tell us, "But that doesn't have the headline where it's supposed to be." It's ingrained. From the academic system, through the military system, to the workplace, the entire country has been taught to conform, to fit in. And I still haven't seen where conforming makes a lot of sense.

The Hungry-Eye Hiring Theory

Anger, passion, need—you want people whose lives are on the line.

At Deutsch, we hire people who are hungry and a little pissed off. That's who we look for: people with something to prove. They know they have the skills to put them at the top of their field, but they haven't quite got there yet. This goes for all corners of the organization; creative or account side, it doesn't matter. In their previous job maybe the boss was never going to move, so they could never move up. I don't want the president of another successful agency to come work for me; I want the executive vice president who hasn't done it yet; this job is going to be the place where she puts her thumbprint. I'm always looking for the passion of the first time. That's when people's soul comes out.

In order to create a place of creativity, you need to be able to spot people with the ability to be creative. That sounds obvious—you can't have a creative environment without creative people—

but you'd be surprised what passes for talent in some offices. The ability to build a creative environment starts with your own creativity.

Certainly there are some people who are just bad. Uncreative, clichéd hacks. It's easy for me to stay away from them; they as much as give off a stale odor. And you can hire people with pedigree. "Let's get the guy who did that commercial that we all liked." He has made his mark. He'll be creative; he's already proved he can be.

But to me, the real G-spot for turbo-creativity is the man or woman who hasn't really accomplished breakthrough work yet but in whom you see a spark. It's in their eyes. Not only will they bring the creative ability you are able to intuit, they will bring the need to prove something to you, to the world, to themselves. They are just almost *there.* There's an extra level of anger, an extra level of passion, an extra level of need—they want their work to be that much better because *they are on the line.*

I want a roomful of gladiators unafraid of convention. Then we throw them in the deep end of the pool. You want a little five percent possibility that they might be in over their head. The guys who built Deutsch's Los Angeles office, my partners out there, two terrific guys, Mike Sheldon and Eric Hirshberg, came to a new agency to try and carve their niche. This was a big moment for them and they created a dynamo operation. Our LA operation is now the industry's third-largest office on the West Coast.

Eight years ago when our creative director left, my immediate impulse was to look outside the company for a new executive. Ultimately, however, I asked Kathy Delaney, who was already with us, to step up to the position on an interim basis. She worked hard, did a great job, and made it permanent. She's brilliant and one of the reasons for our success.

A good boss—an insightful, daring, *fearless* boss—needs to hire people who have never really felt that they're part of the club. You want someone with untapped talent, tremendous confidence, and a string of insecurities. You want people who are constantly willing to scratch and claw, and who, when they succeed, will say, "Yeah, we belong in this club . . . but how did we get here?" Cocky—"We're better than everybody else"—but somehow uncertain of their gifts. "We won. Wow, this is funny."

Though I've hired plenty of people with impressive books, I prefer it when the people I bring in haven't made their bones. I like it when they don't care if nobody's ever done it their way before so long as it gets done their way now. Combine a tremendous pride in the quality of what you do with the humility to pick yourself up when you fail and the balls to get it done, and you've got a job at Deutsch. I want folks hungry. Better: young and hungry and a little pissed off that they haven't made it yet.

We at Deutsch are the quintessential outsiders, which is a good thing to be. We don't carry ourselves like we're the guys on top; we don't seem to own the level of success we've in fact achieved. But we know our strengths. We're scrappers, overachievers, and it's a scrapper's mentality that keeps us edgy. Mike Duda, our head of business development, has a sign on his desk that says it right: "Success is fleeting. Greatness endures."

Look at sports teams. Championships are based on talent, but I always evaluate any sporting matchup on who has more on the line, who has something to prove. In 2004, I looked at the American League and just knew Boston was going to win. If the Yankees didn't win, what was going to happen? They'd have to deal with owner George Steinbrenner. Okay, but they'd still have money in their pocket and twenty-six championship banners on the wall. Boston had two strong assets going. Number one—you could feel it—they had a chemistry, they had a soul. This was a bunch of renegade misfits with a desperado quality to them, all hungry; they hadn't done it before. And, number two, they had a very strong new ingredient, pitcher Curt Schilling. I would have been surprised if this particular team hadn't won.

The 2004 Yankees, having won four World Series between 1996 and 2000, didn't have that hunger. They had a team full of all-stars, but they didn't have a soul. The Yankees won those four World Series because they had a core of Derek Jeter, Andy Pettitte, Mariano Rivera, Paul O'Neill, Scott Brosius, Jorge Posada, and Bernie Williams—homegrown or longtime Yankees who understood the concept of working together toward a common goal. The 2004 team had a collection of excellent athletes but no common emotional cause. They wanted to win, they didn't *need* to win. The Red Sox players had like-minded souls and something to prove. I thought Boston was unbeatable.

Sometimes hunger can backfire and you can want something too much. I have seen desperate books and desperate men. But I try to look beyond desperation to ability. If there is something screaming to get out, I want to be the guy to give it room.

The irony is that people in the advertising industry—and in many other high-visibility, high-dollar fields—are very sheep-like. "Okay, we are only going to hire people from the five best creative agencies." The reality is, half of what makes those people's work good is that they are in the right place at the right time. Many truly talented people have been overlooked or found themselves in the right place on the wrong account. You can find jewels if you have the confidence to hire unpedigreed people. Those are the magical finds.

If tomorrow I brought in the president of Agency X to be president of Deutsch and she came with her own notoriety and established way of doing things, what magic would happen? Whereas if I brought in someone nobody's ever heard of, president of a ten-person agency, then we stand a chance of seeing a light show. You want to find people who are about to begin their career-defining moments and have those moments work for you.

The Doctrine of Female Superiority

Advertising's dirty little secret: Women are better than men.

Women are superior beings. It's that simple. Certainly in business. Give me a choice between a woman and a man with the same talents, I'll take the woman every time. Here's why.

There's so much emotional bullshit that comes with men and the battle for success. We men, the alpha males who fight our way to the top of the business food chain, spend a lot of time worrying about our stripes, about the pelts hanging from our belts. That time could be spent working at our jobs, but no. Our goals include greed and domination. "Why did that guy get the corner office? Why was his raise bigger than mine? I've got to run this place." Size matters.

Women, on the other hand, want to do the job. They want to work in a collaborative environment, they want to succeed, and they want to be paid fairly. This is exactly what you want in a senior executive. No nonsense, just good work and respect.

How did this happen? Watch the commercials on Saturday morning TV; that's where the American socialization process starts, if not before. Advertising is not going to change the deep wiring of what men and women are all about, but it does often serve to perpetuate society's roles. In the advertisements for a doll or a girl's game, there are always three or four girls sitting around in a group, playing, giggling, having fun together. For a boy's toy or game, at the end one boy always wins, shoots his arm in the air and shouts "Yeah!" The other boys are losers. Things go downhill from there.

One of the reasons Deutsch Inc. has been so successful is that I've recognized the superiority of women in business and have consistently put them in positions of responsibility and power. If I put out a job spec for senior people, seven out of ten prospects will be women and the men will always be the weakest candidates. My choices, except as to which of several highly qualified women to promote, are rarely difficult.

The ad business has become increasingly feminized in the last twenty-five years. When I graduated from Wharton in 1979, there were two idiots out of the entire graduating class who went into advertising. I was one of them largely because my father was in the business. Ogilvy & Mather was paying $22,000 a year; Salomon Brothers was starting people off at $75,000. After five years in advertising you could have made $110,000; five years at Salomon Brothers and you could be pulling down a million. You're a business student with a newly minted master's, which industry are you going to join?

Advertising is an industry in which the pay scale is demonstrably lower than that of other professional industries such as banking, real estate, and consulting; women, with far more restricted career options and the upper echelons of fewer industries open to them, entered the field in large numbers and have somehow been able to rationalize the pay scale inequity, look to the future for their earnings, find something other than simply money to work for, and forge successful careers. The pay scale was and continues to be so out of whack that we've lost an entire generation of male business talent; the overwhelming majority of those alpha males are certainly not stampeding into advertising. The ones who do are facing the best women, some of the most talented business-people anywhere. Is it a surprise that women in advertising are succeeding?

Of the ten top executives at Deutsch, eight are women. The two men are spectacular, but guess what, it's eight to two. In our New York office my chief operating officer is a woman, my general manager/director of client services is a woman, my executive creative director is a woman, my chief strategy officer is a woman, my chief financial officer is a woman. We have the best talent pool because, when I was hiring, I wasn't worried about man or woman, I was trying to find the best people—and the best people kept turning out to be women.

Advertising, by its nature, is a more feminine industry than most. It's hard for alpha males, having grown up to be firemen or to fly jet fighters and shoot down enemy aircraft, to do something so personally subservient as service an account. I was always able to do it because I saw the field as a bigger game, but if I hadn't had a family business to go into, I wouldn't have lasted a month.

As men get older, in any service business—and advertising is about as service-oriented as it gets—the job gets more difficult. We need to live more on the content side of the equation, but we are always at the mercy of some guy who tells us we've got to go meet him at his ski house.

I don't know how it happened, I don't know if it started on television with *Bewitched,* but none of the other professions—not investment banking, not consulting, not accounting—comes with the expectation that, in addition to our professional services, we are to provide extensive wining and dining. No matter how good you are—and Deutsch as an agency does as little of that wining and dining as possible—you're still dramatically on the service side of the equation. And after all that, we must always get put into review every three or four years. For an alpha male, that gets very difficult.

If you're a top-shelf heart surgeon, you don't have to talk to anybody. If I sat in that profession where I sit in mine, you wouldn't be able to breathe my air. The top investment bankers, even if they're on the sell side of the equation, carry themselves like kings. In advertising, on the same sell side, you could be the top person in the field, but you still strap on the knee pads.

Yet, Deutsch is a very masculine agency. Obviously there are exceptions to every rule. Two of my partners, Eric Hirshberg and Mike Sheldon, who built the LA office, are stars of the first magnitude and punch holes in my theory. Our female executives don't think of themselves as women first, executives second; they're all hard workers dedicated to the task. In fact, they are all very feminine, beautiful women—but extremely tough. I would put each of them in a street fight with any guy any time. So we have the toughness you need in business added to an essentially collaborative nature. Women are easier to deal with than men, less insecure, more concerned with doing their job and working collaboratively and getting paid fairly.

Basically, less of a pain in the ass.

I gave a presentation to the executive committee of Interpublic, the group that bought Deutsch, in which I discussed our top management. I was talking to eighteen men and one woman. (I suspect she was there because, as with so many committees, they had to have *a* woman.) These were gray and graying men, average age around sixty. I showed slides in which they saw exactly who was involved in running our company and said, "Guys, I'm going to share with you my dirty little politically incorrect secret: Women are superior to men in business. And, I think, in life."

I told them very much what I'm telling you.

After I spoke I didn't know whether they didn't want to hear it, didn't get what I was saying, were taken aback, or were sitting there thinking, "Wow, that's pretty smart." The room was very quiet. The good news is that, since that time, Interpublic has recognized the situation and is now taking an active role in the issue of diversity.

NBC and Donald Trump shot part of the second episode of the first season of *The Apprentice* in our offices. It was classic, a science experiment come to life. The teams were divided eight-on-eight, men versus women. The producer told me, "The women kicked ass yesterday, opening up lemonade stands." I gave them their assignment, to create an advertising campaign for a corporate jet airline. The teams broke away into separate conference rooms to choose team leaders and began to work.

An hour later one of the producers came to me and said, "You are going to crack up." He took me in to see the women. They were sitting around a table, talking, working. They had twenty ideas up on the whiteboard already and were well on their way. Then he took me to the men. The room, which had started out swept clean and ready for action, was full of half-eaten sandwiches and paper bags tossed all over the place. Now, men may be pigs—and I have no problem with that (we are who we are)—but worse than the casual disorder was the fact that they hadn't chosen a team leader yet. They were fighting over who the team leader should be. The question of biggest balls hadn't been decided.

Interestingly, it was the women who played the sex card on that campaign. Their ads were phallic and more than a little obvious, but they were consistent throughout. These were all sexy women and they knew—from firsthand experience, I had a feeling—that sex sells. The men's ads, once they got them going, were well-considered if lacking in some kind of edge. But worse, while the women had been in contact with the owner of the airline to find out what he wanted to emphasize about his company, the men had neglected to cover that base. In all hubris, the men had decided for him. They never thought to ask, "What's a win for you?" That's a major error, and when it came time to pick a winner, I chose the women.

As I usually do.

One of the men got fired as a result. That's the way it works.

The Mutual-Win
Management Formula

If your people feel their win means something to you—that you get actual joy from it—they will walk through fire for you.

One key to running a good organization is having everyone who works there know you care about their wins. Not more than your own, because that makes you a *putz*. Not less, because that makes you a dick. Be happy for your people's success.

To run a good crew you need to put your ego aside for a moment and concentrate on a person other than yourself. For some bosses that's asking too much. Those folks will never have loyal organizations; staff will leave whenever they're offered more money, a better title, more responsibility, an office with a window. More staff will be hired, they'll work for a while, and the pattern will continue forever. Some shops turn over constantly. I wonder why.

For others it comes easy.

How do you know what's a win for someone else? You listen to them, you ask questions, you watch what excites them, you see what leaves them cold. In fact that's a large part of my job; in order to motivate individuals, I have to know them. I am by nature a listener. My tendency, when I meet people, is to ask them about themselves. "What's going on with you?" It's not that I'm such a nice guy; I just naturally do it. Salesmen do this as well.

People enjoy talking about themselves; they often find it flattering to be asked and will warm to the opportunity. And they all have stories. This person doesn't have a family, so her work is going to fill a different space in her life than it would for a woman with a husband and three children. One person's husband doesn't work; she's the main breadwinner in the family and she likes it that way. Another had a tyrannical father and is looking to the workplace to provide a peaceful family system. It's remarkable what you as a good listener will piece together if you pay attention to your workers the same way you do to a friend or a spouse.

For example, our head of business development, Mike Duda. He works on commission and I cracked up when I saw the figures and realized how much money he made last year. I don't begrudge him a penny; the more he made the more we made. But I also saw that earning a ton of dough wasn't his goal. I'm sure he liked it, I'm sure he preferred making a fabulous living over working for nothing, but money is not what drives him. What became clear when I saw what made him happy was that a win for Mike would be to be a leader in business. He told me he wants to run a business one day; that's what turns him on. Whether running a huge part of Deutsch, running another agency, or coming up with a new business model and owning his own shop, Mike's got influence on his mind. He wants to be a leader in this business; that's what makes him tick.

Deutsch has approximately one thousand employees and Mike is among the top ten most important people who define the agency and make it go. I look to him as one of the two or three people whom I will ask for big business opinions: not "Do you like this ad," but "Should we open an office in Atlanta?" or "Should we pitch that piece of business?" That's what turns him on. And knowing that he is growing and feels vested makes my job and life easier and happier. I couldn't be happier for him, and he knows it.

Some people are stingy with their compliments. They feel that a paycheck is statement enough that an employee is appreciated at his work. A friend of mine runs a garment business. One year I told him that Deutsch had been so successful we had given out millions in end-of-year bonuses. He said, "You know what my people's bonus is? They can come to work January 1. That's their bonus, they still have their jobs." Garmento mentality, comes out of a generation that survived the Great Depression and handed down that eternal fear to their children and grandchildren.

What signal does his kind of tightness send to his workers? That their work is important to him? That their effort is appreciated? That they're not there just to serve his goals? No. My friend was as much as telling them that they're machines and could be replaced. Do you think, when he needs them to put in extra effort to get an order out, they'll stay a second after the bell rings at five to lend a hand? Nope, there'll be tumbleweed blowing down the main street of that town.

My father is a wonderful man outside the office. I love him tremendously. He has the aesthetic of an artist, which he is; he is as honest as any man I've ever met; his work ethic is second to none, and he has a great human respect for people. He was completely nurturing to me. I could strike out in Little League ten times in a row and he'd come down from the stands after the game and tell me, "Great job, Donny," make me feel like I was not a failure, and mean it. My dad was the best man at my wedding. He has my back like nobody else in the world, and I have his the same way.

My dad built David Deutsch Associates from one room and a telephone. He did the hard part; he built something from nothing. He had the skill set and the balls and the determination to open the door. I don't know that I could have done what he did. My dad was an art director by trade; a perfectionist, he would spend four hours moving a piece of type around. He built his business around his personality; refined, conservative, quiet.

Yet, as a boss, if he had one shortcoming—compared to my *many* shortcomings—sometimes he ruled with an iron hand and didn't see the big picture. One of the three big fights we had in ten years of business together—a real screaming match—was over how to handle an art director with a messy work space. My father was meticulous in his neatness; to him, a sloppy office was the sign of a sloppy mind. One young art director's office was a pigsty, work strewn all around; you could barely walk inside. The guy had a folded-up futon in there. Why? Because some nights he worked so late he slept on it.

One day I walked in and found my father screaming at this kid: "Clean it up. You can't work here and have an office like that. Get this futon out of here!" I asked my dad to join me in his own office. I closed the door and said, "Dad, you're yelling at this kid who's got a bed in his office. Think about how absurd that is. You're as much as saying to this kid, 'Don't work as hard.' " My father had a blind spot.

So I pay a lot of attention to the things people who work for me want for themselves. Often it's money. It's been said that money is how we keep score. Well, for some folks that's true, which is why for years at Deutsch we ran this competition that I called Cash Wingo. We would be pitching an account, let's say it was a $30 million account that was going to pay the agency $4 million a year in fees. I would gather the four top people who were going to drive this pitch, and tell them, "Okay—*Cash Wingo!* We get this, the four of you split $200,000. You guys decide how you're going to split it." (I knew they'd split it evenly, but that was my way of saying, "You're pirates. Here's your pot of gold.")

Sounds like a lot of money to leave as a carrot, but to me it was a no-brainer. The company gets $4 million a year for as long as we keep the account; I'm giving our best people a shot at five percent of the first year's income. To us it's a tax-deductible incentive; to them it's a bonanza. "Wow, I can take that vacation. Wow, if I do this I can buy a new Mercedes!"

There's something about money as a motivator. A weird dynamic takes over: whether you're wealthy or need money desperately, everybody wants that Cash Wingo. It's about the greenbacks; when you attach money to an equation, something extra-special happens. People will work extra-hard to nail down that $50K.

For some people money doesn't change the molecular equation. For them it's all about the win, or creating the product, or the good feeling of engaging in high-level competition. In business it's easy to forget there are rewards other than the monetary. In this same case, in fact, I made a huge mistake. We won that very large piece of business and they got their Cash Wingo, so I was surprised when two or three of my most important people came into my office with their heads down.

"What's up, guys?"

"You didn't even tell us 'Great job.' "

I'd forgotten. I don't give myself a big hug after we win an account; I'm looking several steps down the line to *How do we get this campaign done?* But my colleagues aren't me. I should know that.

That's one of my faults as a manager; the people whom I respect the most, the folks whom I truly think of as my family, my brethren, are the people I treat the worst. Because I respect them so much, because they are so much a part of who I am, because I see them as true equals—and because I don't give *myself* a lot of hugs—I forget they have emotional needs. Did I forget to say it? Did I not tell them I love them loudly enough? I guess I did. My fault.

I do this pretty consistently. And every time I apologize, I try to explain myself: "I'm actually showing you the ultimate sign of respect, because I don't think you need that. You're with me and we're in this together, and we're just thinking, 'What's next?' " They laugh at me. I'm wrong. It's a flaw, one of many, and it's been called to my attention and I'm working on it. From the earliest age, from the toughest to the not tough at all, we all need to be told, "You did good. Thank you."

You need some of that; you need the hugs and the compliments. But you need balance. I'm still learning. I was in my office meeting with my top staff when word came that we had won *Adweek*'s Agency of the Year for the fourth time in five years. I turned and said "Great," then went right back to the work at hand. I didn't share that jug with enough enthusiasm. I should have taken a big swig and passed it around; it would have tasted good to everyone. "I recognize how great you are and the job you've done" must meet "There's more to be done."

As a boss, you need to be aware of the power of your own words. In 2002 we had a big pitch for Monster.com, the online employment network. They were looking for a new agency and it was down to us, Saatchi & Saatchi, and Doyle Dane Bernbach.

The form of an advertising presentation doesn't vary much. The first forty minutes is your strategic setup. You analyze the client's business and bring to the table the data from your amalgamation of qualitative, quantitative, and secondary research, all the block-and-tackle analysis of information that's in the marketplace that can help. You then use your own brain to, first, advise them what positions not to take, and then, arrive at your strategic position: "Here's where you want to position the brand." Then you say, "Here's the creative idea," and articulate the position. The creative person stands up and shows storyboards and print ads and videos and wows them. After that is the media presentation, which boils down to "Okay, if your budget is $90 million, here's how we think you should spend it." We use our research and know-how to map out a spending plan that involves, say, twenty percent on television, including a breakout for cable versus broadcast TV; thirty percent on magazines, and here's where and why; fifteen percent outdoors. . . . You basically slice and dice their budget so they can get where they need to go and get the greatest exposure and the biggest bang for the buck.

The current buzzword in advertising is *integration* of all consumer touchables. Forty or fifty years ago you did a radio ad, a TV ad, and a magazine ad, and that was it. Today there's all of that plus the Internet, direct mail, public relations, sales promotion; and all avenues intersect. How do we get Monster's message out there so it's completely uniform and each piece is working together? Other agencies have a direct-mail division, an interactive division, a public-relations division, and they're all siloed; they don't talk to each other and they're fighting each other for money. At Deutsch we have all those departments, but we are still one company, one profit center. Our innovative, seamless approach allows us to work compatibly, efficiently, and productively, which we explain at this point in every pitch.

Our creative department presented the line "Today's the day." It positioned Monster to stand for empowerment; you can seize the day when you "Have a Monster Day." It was a call to action. *Today's the day* you can find a job. *Today's the day* you can upgrade your skills. *Today's the day* you can network with new people. *Today's the day* you can change your life. We made Monster.com into a way of life, an ethos. An excellent line: Today's the day.

In the last part of the presentation, the media, we show how we take our idea and blow it out across all the disciplines. "You'll love this campaign: *Today's the Day*. Here's how it works on the Internet . . ." We redesigned their Web site to encompass it. We have a fine media department but historically the media part of the presentation is not what drives the win.

A pitch usually takes between two and three hours. Usually the client falls in love with the creative and that carries the day. This time they said, "We love the direct-response part. We love the strategic part. The media ideas blew us away." During one of the breaks, however, one of Monster's representatives said, "We love everything. We're not sure about the creative. We don't know if it's breakthrough enough." I tried to reassure him, but I didn't know whether I succeeded.

After every new business meeting, I gather my head people and debrief them, try to learn from the day, consolidate our gains and improve our skills for next time. In front of our interactives, our media people, our direct-response folks, everyone, I said, "This is amazing. This is how far we've come as an agency, that we don't even need the creative to win anymore. The creative actually missed a little bit on this one."

The meeting was over and Kathy Delaney, our creative director, who is tough as nails, came into my office, crying. "How could you? All the creative work I ever did . . ." She was devastated.

And rightly so. I had made a terrible mistake. I held Kathy in such high regard that I thought she would understand that, in order to elevate the rest of the staff, I could throw her to the wolves a little bit without damaging her standing in the company. That's what I thought I'd been doing.

But I'd been incredibly insensitive. Kathy is my rock but she still has an ego, she's a human being, she's fragile. I'd made a personal and a management mistake. I tell Kathy she's great all the time; I thought she knew I meant it.

People tell me regularly, "Hey, Donny, you don't know how much your approval means. You don't know how strong your words are. Give that person a hug." My father never told anyone, "Good job," because he expected their best, and it cost him. This time it cost me, too. I apologized to Kathy and told her how much I loved and respected her. I thought my hugs were so evident, but I guess they weren't. It's something I'm working on.

Monster called us to their offices later that week. "We want all your people in the room." We walked in and they told us, "Have a Monster day!" We got the business.

How wrong I had been. The client ended up loving the campaign and used it for the next four years.

This time I thanked Kathy personally.

The Great Disappearing-Boss Doctrine

"If you want something done right, do it yourself." *Wrong.* Show the confidence to be the guy not needed.

The impulse to put your fingerprints on everything is very strong: you're running the show, so run it! Any organization needs the clarity of single-minded decision making. An organization gets in trouble when there's waffling and politics and it's not clear who's in charge. Even when you have a group dynamic and great collaboration, at the end of the day there always needs to be one tiebreaker.

However, and this may seem like a paradox but it's not, there is a lot to be said for judiciously delegating your authority. To do so you have to come to terms with two guiding principles: One, your ego has to be sufficiently intact for you not to be needed; two, you must understand and accept that when someone else acts on your behalf, all you can expect is that they operate at your quality level, not that they will do things exactly your way.

Many small businesses never get past being small because the people who run them never allow anyone else near the power source. The guy whose business stays small believes he is, or more accurately, *wants to be* needed at every meeting. He'll complain, "Clients—oh, shit, I've gotta be there." Yet on some level he wants it that way. He's unwilling or unable to reach the point where he can say with ease, "The client didn't ask for me? They're okay with all those other people and not me? Great!" When you're smart enough to pat yourself on the back for creating an organization that brings in work, makes money, and frees you to do more of the same, then you've turned a management corner.

"If you want something done right, do it yourself." *Wrong.* That's hard for some people to let go of. They see the world one way—theirs—and accept no substitutes. Any diversion from their absolute standards brings discontent, if not outright hostility.

It is unreasonable to expect a business associate to be your clone. In fact, it is a mathematical certainty that their final work— their creation—and yours will not be the same. You'll probably think theirs is five percent worse than yours, it may even be five percent better, but that's not the point. To grow an organization you need to allow—encourage!—your teams to own their work completely. Their work will grow when it's theirs; it will wither if it's constantly criticized as less than yours. At that point you will either stunt your people or lose them, and you'll be smaller as a result. You have to come to terms with that, or your business will remain at whatever level it is today.

Several years ago a young guy, Eric Hirshberg, interviewed for the job of creative director at our new Los Angeles office. He had been creative director at a small agency without a great reputation and there were only one or two interesting pieces of work in his book. What I liked about the guy was the fire and passion in his eyes. This was a kid who didn't know what he didn't know. Very brash. Loved advertising and was doing what he loved every day.

You want a guy like that on your team, so I hired him and threw him into the deep end of the pool.

Eric had a very strong sense of himself. Like me, he had a big ego. He was the kind of guy who needed to raise his hand and say, "I did that!"—and that's a good thing. After a while his work more than progressed; it became truly brilliant. In a very short time, all the clients in the LA office wanted Eric all the time.

Mitsubishi was my biggest client. It was a driving part of the LA office and I was completely involved in the work. The campaign became one of our signature successes. We had a brilliant team running it—Eric doing creative, Mike Sheldon on the business end—but I was still the go-to guy who gave the big-deal presentations in front of six hundred dealers. One day I got a call from the head client, who told me, "Hey, Donny, you don't have to come to the next Vegas show. Eric's a great presenter. Let Eric present."

I felt a quick lump in my chest. "Huh?" But in the next second I thought, "Great! I don't have to go to Vegas!" That show was always a grueling nonstop business grind and I was rarely happy to be there. The account was in good hands and I was now freed to pursue other goals.

I knew Eric liked being at the center of things—he's got a big presence—but after a while he started complaining. "Every client wants me and I have to be everywhere!" The small-business mentality. I told him, "Of course they do, Eric. You're a great presenter and if you're in the room next to a guy who's your subordinate, they're always going to say, 'Yeah, I want Eric.' You're where you are for a reason.

"But you see what I did with you? You do brilliant work and the agency gets credit for it. You need to repeat the same math. The game for you now is, How do I find people so that I am not needed? You need to hire people as good as, if not better than, you are. Don't be afraid of the guy who's got twenty years' experience and is even more credentialed. You find amazing people, they work for you, and their work falls under your domain, the Eric Hirshberg portfolio, and you're that much smarter as a result.

"All these people that you're going to bring in will be able to do the work that will be put in front of the client. And they're not Eric! The client would probably rather have Eric, but they'll be happy with who you send them. *You need to be comfortable enough not to be needed.*" He seemed to be absorbing what I was saying.

"I'm going to tell you a dirty little secret," I said. "When you do that, you'll feel ten levels of joy more than if you presented your work yourself. They're going to have their fingerprints all over the work—they're going to do it, it's going to be theirs—but you will still be one percent of those people's successes. You'll still have something they don't; you'll have more vision about how all the pieces fit into the whole, and you will have set them on the path.

"It also helps the work," I told him. "Because you're not the line guy, you're in a position to solve problems if things go bad. You can separate yourself from the process. Let's say the client's not happy. If you're the person doing the work, there's no place for them to go. Now, with some distance, you can arrive and say, 'Let me step in and fix it.' You're more effective in that role. You can spend ten percent of the time and be fifty percent more effective."

It took a couple of years. During that time the LA office built its credits and client list with a great creative department and incredibly talented people. Ultimately, I got the call.

"Donny," said Eric, "I gotta tell you. I sat in a meeting with Coors and my team this morning. I know I got the work to where it needed to be—I gave them the spark. I had my hands on it, but I didn't. It was theirs, they took it from start to finish . . . and it felt great! The client doesn't seem to need me at every meeting. I got such joy out of seeing what they were able to accomplish and knowing I helped them get there. And, boy, you are so right about that feeling—it is magical!"

And I got even more joy: theirs, his, and my own.

My social science experiment worked. I firmly believe that if people have the tools—if they are bright enough, tough enough, hungry enough—if you throw them in the deep end of the water, you get greatness. Hire good people, train them, then let them do their jobs. Not that they needed me to tell them.

The Boss-Subordinate Role Model

Have the strength to let people get upset at you.

People get pretty caught up in their jobs. If you really put yourself into your work, I don't see how that doesn't happen. We're not sleepwalking through our tasks; they're important and we're trying to do them the best way we know how. Sometimes, however, tunnel vision can take on a life of its own. My early experience with the coffee experts at Ogilvy, twenty grown men sitting around talking passionately about a three-second sliver of a commercial, gave me a glimpse of how far out there some people can get. Every once in a while we'll be in a meeting passionately arguing about, let's say, what music we should use on the soundtrack of a commercial. People get upset, they get fried, they start to unravel. Arguments get personal and cosmic. At that point, I've just got to say, "Guys, let's remember what we're doing. We're not curing cancer here."

Meltdowns happen. I play the boss-subordinate role quite often. There isn't a person at Deutsch who doesn't know they work for me; there's no doubt anywhere about who's in charge. But I allow people to melt down on me. They can go at me, they can call me a moron, they can tell me, "I can't believe how you fuckin' handled that situation." No more or less than I would say to them.

In fact, every boss needs to have at least one person—and, hopefully, a bunch of people—in the organization who will call him on his bullshit. I have found that truly strong leaders like and respect it. They are refreshed by informed candor. They almost long for the person who can say to them, "Let me tell you what I think." They rarely get that. It's nice to be surrounded by yes-people, folks who tell you how smart you are. But I have found my biggest growing experiences have come from the Linda Sawyers, Val DiFebos, Kathy Delaneys, Mike Sheldons, Eric Hirshbergs, who will call me on my stuff. It makes me better and allows me to make them better.

They can't melt down on me in front of other people; that could cause rebellion in the ranks and is over the line; but I understand that people get involved in what they're doing—I certainly do—and sometimes stuff comes out of their mouths that they regret almost immediately. Recognizing this counts for a lot. They get chits and they appreciate my being calm when they're steamed.

Again, I know the feeling; I had a big screaming match with one client and wound up telling him I thought he was bipolar. That violates every tenet of Working with Clients 101 and was just remarkably stupid. To this day the man brings it up. But that time he was the one who got chits. That guy let me tell him he was insane and he didn't fire me; I owe him one.

It's important to maintain your composure. People want strength. When you're in a position of power, you can't show vulnerability; that will ruin you. You've got to be The Guy. Late one hot August afternoon, two years after 9/11, I was working in the office when all of a sudden the power went out. Okay, I figured, brownout. A few seconds went by and the lights didn't come back on. I saw all these little heads pop up around me. I could see fear, particularly in the young people; their minds were going immediately to terrorism. These are the times we live in. From our balcony we could see a big, black cloud of smoke rise from across town. Fifteen minutes later the transistor radios in the office brought news that it was a citywide blackout. I saw panic creep across some faces.

As boss and leader, I couldn't let them see me sweat. I didn't have any special hot line to the mayor's office, I didn't know anything more than anyone else, but they were looking to me for leadership and I gave it to them. I walked around the office, chatting with people along the way, letting them see me smile. I didn't show vulnerability. When you were little, you never wanted to see your daddy cry. As the afternoon passed I even made a little joke: "Okay, if anybody wants to consummate any office relationships, now's the time to do it!" Sooner or later I sent them all home early.

When we've presented a pitch and I've been uncertain that we were on the winning track, have I let on to the troops? Never. Often wrong, never in doubt. We lose a pitch and I feel like crying. No. I've got to be the one who says, "Fuck them. They made a mistake." That's what people depend on me for, that's what they are looking for me to do, that's what a leader does.

While you should never show vulnerability, you can show that you need help. A boss can show frustration, you can let people see human flaws, and to me there's a difference. We all have our moments of weakness, no question about that, and it empowers your people to help you on a specific problem or task.

I've had people break down in front of me—it usually happens with women, but I've had men cry as well—when they feel I've been too tough on them. Perspective is vital. I tell them, "There is nothing happening in this place, or will ever happen in this place, that is worth crying about." They look at me, somewhat relieved. "Ultimately in life you will have things to cry about. They ain't here."

Sometimes You Have to Be a Dickhead

I don't care how motivated a worker is, he will take it up a notch when the boss is on a rampage. That's just the way it is.

When I was younger I was pretty mercurial. I would fly off the handle; my moods would swing up and down and so would my volume. I was a volatile guy and I was not above raising the decibel level to make my point. Okay, I was a screamer. As I've aged and become more successful, as I've gotten more sure of who I am and who I'm not, I've tended to talk a little softer. I don't need the volume as much anymore, or the bravado.

But sometimes you do need to raise your voice. I'm not a screamer by nature, but often it happens organically in response to some crisis or incident or bonehead play. The worst fights I've had have been with the press, who, because of the Bad Boy persona they participated in creating, have come to expect it. I've had some brutal screaming matches with Alison Fahey, editor of *Adweek*—yelling, screaming, hanging up the phone. She's a brilliant journalist and has been a good friend to the agency, but we've gone at it to the point where we didn't talk for a few months. I've told *The New York Times,* "Blow me!" (though, in my defense, I was kidding around and that was said and received in good fun) and lived to tell.

Volume and four-letter words, there's not a lot attached to it with me; it's the way I communicate. I can just scream through people and then it's done. The people who work for me have figured that out. I would never yell at a junior kid, I wouldn't dress down someone in front of other people; you're just a bully at that point. But I will yell at a group and expect to see results.

Sometimes I do it for effect. In 1996 Deutsch was going through a dry spell. Over the period of a couple of months we hadn't won a pitch and I wasn't feeling the energy from any part of the organization that we needed to succeed. Why the hell not? I got all the senior partners in one room, the entire group, and lit into them.

"Guys, we're not as good as we think we are," I began. There wasn't spit flying out of my mouth, but I started at a pretty good volume level and kept on cranking. "We've lost the fire. We're reading too much of our own press." I took apart the organization for a minute and then went around the room, person by person, and dressed down each one of my top people. This wasn't individual, this was universal; everybody there needed a wake-up call and it had to be both corporately generic and very personal. Keep in mind they were all brilliant, but I felt that we as a group had gotten complacent. This was my way of challenging them.

"Steve, when was the last breakthrough media idea you had?

"Esther, you're doing new business, when was the last time you took a fresh look at our credentials presentation?

"Greg, the creative is too narrow. When are you going to take a wider view and broaden it?

"Cheryl, strategic ideas. You're starting to work out of a formula. You're working out of a formulated box. When was the last breakthrough strategic idea you had?"

I could see on their faces that I had unsettled them. Had I gone too far?

I sensed that maybe I was taking them down one notch too low, though there's nothing wrong with that. People should be made to feel accountable. "There's nobody in this room who is not to blame." Then I started yelling at myself. "To tell you the truth, I don't think *I*'m on my best game, so I'm partially angry at myself. I'm not thinking out of the box lately. I'm doing what I always did; I'm not pushing myself to the next level and wherever that takes me. So maybe I'm mad at myself, okay? I'm mad at everybody else, too."

I'm a very self-motivated guy, but I find when someone comes at me, it takes me up a notch. I'll either say, "Fuck you, I'm on my A game!" or "Fuck you, you're right!" No matter who we are, we don't always go at 100 rpm. At one point or another we all need a little kick in the ass, even if we have to do it ourselves.

I heard about that meeting for a year afterward. "He came in and told us we really sucked and we walked out and we're saying, like, 'Fuck him.' " But they did get more intense about their work, and the work did improve.

I find that when people think the boss is really on edge, really flying off the handle, something happens. You can't do it all the time; you can't even do it regularly. No good boss wants to be a tyrant; ruling by fear can be counterproductive. But I don't care how motivated a worker is, he will take it up to the next notch when the boss is pissed and on a rampage. That's just the way it is.

I find the best kind of manager has the same qualities that make a great parent: loving, but very tough; nurturing, but demanding. She's a strong disciplinarian, but the kids know she loves them and has their best interests at heart. That's the formula: incredible caring about the entire place as if it were a family, caring about individual people within that family, but not suffering fools gladly.

You're really not supposed to scream at the clients. I've broken that rule, too. Not often, but sometimes it's been necessary. Again, I would never raise the volume with a client in front of his people or mine, but one-on-one you can get loud if there's enough at stake. In fact, if you make your case strongly enough, people give you passion points.

One of the top executive vice presidents at Mitsubishi thought one of my guys was going around him to his boss. He called and threatened us. I went off on the guy.

"You're out of your mind! I've been nothing but loyal to you. This is not the way we do things. You know that. I'm insulted! I don't deserve that at this point, with what I've gone through with you! That's unacceptable!" I was very heated in defense of my guy and my company.

You can't do that very often, but in the end, if you're steamed but rational, clients will respect you. Think of any important relationship you've had in your life, whether it's with a child, a spouse, a parent, a business partner, an employee. At some point there's been a raising of voices . . . because there's a lot at stake. And sometimes you just have to be a dickhead about it.

The
Ad
World

Selling in the New Millennium: The Brand-Ethos Model

A brand doesn't sell a product, it presents an ethos. A sneaker company shows an eighty-five-year-old man doing push-ups. That campaign says we value the passion that keeps an old man vibrant. We value vibrant people. And how does a consumer who wants to be vibrant react? He says, "I want to sing that anthem, I want to wrap myself in that religion."

And he buys those sneakers.

Many agencies create spots. Commercials. What separates Deutsch and a handful of agencies from the rest of the industry is that we develop a central premise about the brand or product, an ethos, a values-based platform that guides the entire campaign. The commercial is incidental.

There's a process. Our research first produces an insight about the target, the category, or the product itself. Then, before we put the first actor on-screen or the first animator picks up her pixels, we create an ethos, an anthem, a religion, that defines the product we are presenting to the public.

For example, we worked on a campaign for Monster.com, the e-employment agency, a company that was about finding jobs online. As they developed they began to branch out into the moving business and they were looking ahead to more. Our challenge was, How do we define the company as the leader in getting jobs on-line, which they were, and also give them a little bit more of a forward-thinking position, and then incorporate their other businesses and still hit the emotional nerve?

The concept we came up with was "Today's the Day!" It was not about jobs, it was not about moving. Monster the brand would stand for the one vehicle, the one instrument to go to when you're ready to change your life. When you're ready to find the next great job, find the next great home and move into it. Monster.com. That's the ethos of that brand: Today's the day.

That ad ran during the Super Bowl.

Our creative director, Kathy Delaney, came up with the concept, and I think it's brilliant. When someone logs onto Monster, whether they're looking for a waitress job or a bump up to executive, they are making an emotional statement to themselves: "I am not putting anything off, I'm trying to better myself right now. Today's the day." It truly is an example of a brand living in a bigger place than the services it provides.

We were asked to create pro bono advertising for the Partnership for a Drug-Free America. They wanted to target young people who were in the middle of deciding whether or not they were going to do dope, and move them to pass it by. We could simply have created a spot that advised these kids to just say no, but was that going to have the proper effect? Probably not. Who could reach them?

Our research showed that a large percentage of these target children came from single-parent homes in which the mothers were the major influences on family life and life in general. But how much were the kids actually listening? Our research also showed that these women were having a hard enough time making their own way in the world, let alone making it easier for their children. Drugs are very seductive; who says their kids would respond to a word they had to say? Before the mothers could have the power to influence their children, they needed to be respected in their own right.

We came up with the idea to empower these women. That was the central theme: Empower the mothers; then they would guide the kids from a position of respect.

What power could they reasonably be given? Control of their home ground.

The families were largely urban and our campaign put the women in charge of their own children by putting them in charge of the entire block. We made the community and their family one and gave them the power to clean it up one block at a time.

The spot shows the inner city: 143rd Street; Bronx, New York. The streets. A bodega. A fire hydrant. Urban faces. Cops in uniform entering an apartment building. In a playground, kids are playing basketball and jumping double Dutch jump rope. Some adults are playing with them. As the spot progresses the kids smile more often. An African-American woman with a strong face looks directly into the camera. She speaks in a voice-over.

"My name is Elana Olby. I see my family out there. These are my children. They're all my kids. They may not be my children biologically, but they are still my family."

The film shows crack vials scattered on pavement.

"This playground used to be infested, but now my children have a place to play. We bond together and we take care of the problem. See, once you have a family bond, it's like nothing can break through that. It's worth the effort. Long as there's breathing life in this neighborhood, it's worth the effort.

"We are watching.

"This is my block. This is my family."

That was more than a spot; that was a place for an idea to live.

The ethos approach finds a quality in a brand that is greater than its ingredients or attributes. Some other product can always take an ingredient or attribute claim away from you. If you have Stain–Zero that gets clothes clean, someone can always have new Ultrafuron that gets clothes cleaner. If you have a 25,000-mile motor oil, someone can come out with a motor oil with Moto-Run 100K that keeps your motor going smoother longer. Someone can always out-attribute you. Great brands, great advertising, present an ethos, a religion, that people see and go, "Yes. Got that. I like the way you think. You and I are on the same page. Let's go." And the bond of thinking alike, of seeing the world of laundry or the universe of car care the same way, is stronger and lasts longer than any ingredient.

Coors beer ran a series of tremendously successful commercials around the concept of "Wingman," a pal who sacrifices his time and dignity by chatting up some annoyingly self-involved woman so his buddy can be alone with her friend, the girl of his dreams. What does that really have to do with beer? Nothing directly. What works about it? Well, the Coors target consumer is the young guy. He sees that scene and says, "They get me. They get my life, they get what I'm all about! How cool is that?! That moves me. I'll order a Coors and make a statement that I am a rock-on kind of guy." And what is Coors saying? "We understand you, Mr. Twentysomething Beer Drinker, better than anybody else, and here is a little salutation to you and the way you look at the world. You and I are on the same team. We're sharing an ethos. We're sharing a *guy* ethos."

Yes. Let's go.

It's brilliant.

Most of the research we do for our clients is to answer this basic question: What, in reality, *is* this brand? Not just the ingredients inside the box but the essence of the brand itself. If you can isolate a brand's DNA, you can put it directly in touch with the people who will respond to it best.

How do we do this?

We start as close to the brand as we can get. First, we visit the client's operation, talk to the people who work there, dig into the history of the company and the brand.

When we visited LensCrafters for the first time, in the early '90s, they were advertising one-hour service and fifty percent–off sales. We discovered a company of caring people, deeply involved in their Gift of Sight program, which dispenses free eyeglasses to needy people in the U.S. and around the world. They gave away over twenty-five thousand pairs of glasses a year and they held a competition to choose who in the company would have the privilege of going on these missions.

LensCrafters collected and refurbished old frames in every store. It also created careers for, and bettered the lives of, the people behind the counter. As a result, these folks had a passion for what they did that amazed us.

None of that was coming through in their advertising.

We decided the brand positioning was not about fast, cheap eyewear but was really about *eye care*. The first spots featured a real LensCrafters doctor talking about helping people see better, lens technicians discussing fashioning eyewear for a ten-month-old baby, and stylists expressing their passion for helping people to look great in their glasses. The tag line was "LensCrafters. Helping People See Better One Hour at a Time." The new work increased sales ten percent in the first year and the company experienced double-digit growth year after year through the end of the millennium.

Sometimes you have to borrow interest from something that surrounds the brand, because the brand itself just doesn't have sizzle.

The California Milk Advisory Board wanted to promote cheese made in California. At first glance, there's just not that much about cheese that's exciting. It's cheese. However, there's a lot that's exciting about California. Great weather, great babes, a New Age–no-sweat attitude. Between California and cheese, we chose California.

And so was born the "Happy Cows" campaign. California cows have bummer flashbacks about their miserable winter days in old Wisconsin. California cows "hit snooze" when the rooster crows. California cows are the babes of the cow world.

Two bulls are standing in a beautiful, green field, the yellow sun making the colors warm and brilliant. It's milking time. A cow sashays by, her udders full. Very full. One bull says to the other, "Oh yeah, those are real." And then the tag line: "Great Cheese comes from Happy Cows. Happy Cows come from California."

The Happy Cows were a real hit, with T-shirts and plushies and cookbooks and aprons selling like crazy off the Real California Cheese Web site. Sales shot up and our budget increased year after year.

Finding a brand's soul takes some digging and some real strategic thinking, but researching what consumers think about brands is even trickier. There are two main types of research: quantitative and qualitative.

Quantitative research is vital in managing a business and finding out how familiar people are with your brand or your ads. It answers all those questions about when people first used your product, how many times they buy it versus competitors' brands, and how they rate it on things like quality and value. These studies ask hundreds of people fairly simple questions. If you do the studies right, with a good research supply company, and you talk to enough people, you can find out how your customers and prospects are behaving in the marketplace and what they're thinking when they decide which brand to buy. You can compare the behavior and attitudes of men and women, the young and old, frequent buyers and infrequent buyers.

It's important to talk to brand rejecters, too; people who have chosen not to use your product and are buying the competition's. "Why haven't you bought this? Why are you buying the other?" These are the people you need to reach, the people you need to turn around. Listen to them.

Segmentation research divides customers and prospects according to their attitudes toward your category of products, and also according to the main needs they're looking to fill. Research companies make a ton of money selling this information, but it's only worth the dollars if you can figure out how and where to reach each of those attitude groups with a tailored advertising message.

If you do a pharmaceutical segmentation, for example, no matter what disease you're talking about, there are always groups called something like the Worriers, the Copers, the Actives, and the Deniers. You may have paid a million dollars for this information, but unless you know these folks' street addresses or what radio station they listen to in the morning, it does you no good. If you can find out how to reach these people, you can use direct mail, the Internet, events, doctor's office posters, or other marketing tools to get them a relevant message. (To this end, there is at least one company beginning to deliver what it calls "targeted customized television advertising." Their technology is still in the test stage, but ultimately it promises to do on TV essentially what magazines can do in print: send different versions of your advertising to different cities, zip codes, and eventually households.)

At Deutsch, we have a motto: Advertise to the similarities, market to the differences. Wrap your mass advertising around consistencies among consumers, and use other pieces of the marketing mix to customize.

Qualitative research is a whole different operation. It tries to get at how people *feel* about brands. This is one of the most abused kinds of market research around, and the focus group is the most abused form of qualitative.

We do most of our qualitative research ourselves, rather than farm the work out. We prefer small gatherings. Five people is great, seven is the max. Often the client gets nervous with a small sampling, but when you get ten people in a room, you've created an unwieldy group: two are sure to hang back and not speak, interviewers are prevented from getting to know the consumers in the kind of depth we need, and because people are less comfortable talking to a large group, answers tend to be more superficial.

Our groups are preinterviewed, so each person is there with an opinion to offer, not just because they want the money they're being paid. And we don't just talk, talk, talk. These days people who show up at focus groups, and a lot of people in general, are starting to sound like marketers. They toss around words like "target segment" and "benefit" and "brand image." So we make them use the nonverbal side of their brains to reveal what they really feel about a brand. We use a lot of projective techniques: we have them draw pictures of themselves before and after using the product; we put out a big stack of photos and have them choose the pictures they feel show different brands' users, and then explain their choices to the group.

It throws people off. They're prepared with their marketing answers and they remember tag lines, but when we use visuals, they're forced to use a new vocabulary of pictures and we can learn a lot more about what they're really thinking.

People in focus groups give you answers they think you want to hear. They want to come in and sound smart, which is not at all in your best interest. There's an old advertising story, probably apocryphal, about a focus group for a cigarette that was about to be launched. They showed the group two campaigns. One said, "This is a new cigarette that tastes better and lasts longer than any other." The other said, "Here's a campaign that shows a cowboy." All the participants said, "A cowboy? What does he know? A cowboy selling cigarettes? Ridiculous." They went for the conventional. They'd seen it before.

Fortunately for Marlboro, the agency didn't listen to that group.

One technique that came into play in focus groups about twenty years ago and has taken over the research planet is called "laddering." It is about as dangerous to the field of advertising as global warming is to the ice caps. Typically, in a qualitative research session, the moderator will ask a consumer why she likes a certain product. The consumer will say something along the lines of, "I like this product because it gets grass stains out of my laundry." The moderator will then ask, "What's good about that?"

"Well, the clothes look as good as new."

"What's good about that?"

"It gives me pleasure when I fold them."

"What's good about that?"

"I feel like a good mom."

"What's good about that?"

"I know my days on earth have meaning." (In truth, not one member of a focus group has actually said that, but you get the idea.)

Researchers love to get to "the emotional end-end benefits." And as they march up the benefit ladder, as it's called, the end-end is almost always the same: Freedom, happiness, sex. Across categories, every pharmaceutical product, laundry detergent, frozen food, will get you to the same place. Doesn't matter if it's banks or arthritis medicines or airlines, if you follow that reasoning, all the advertising will look exactly the same, because some researcher laddered up from investing safely, following your doctor's advice, or buying a ticket online and got to hopes and dreams and walking on the beach with your grandson.

At Deutsch, we go *down* the benefit ladder and dig into why Brand A can talk about itself in a different language than Brand B. "How are the values built into Brand B different from, how are they similar to, your values, Ms. Consumer?"

How do we learn about someone's values and the way they affect their life and purchases? Sometimes we interview people in their homes or their cars or go to stores and shop with them. We observe a lot and talk very little.

When we worked on a pain reliever, for example, we hired outside anthropologists to be our researchers. They approached pill takers as a subculture. "Aspirin in the Antipodes." They went into people's homes, asked some questions, but more important, opened their kitchen drawers and medicine cabinets and noted details like how the pills were lined up. Whether by size of bottle or pill, time of day to be taken, or strength of pain relief, what stood out was the order their medications imposed on the way these folks lived. People who are on a lot of prescription meds, our anthropologists discovered, are really into their routine and their schedule; it became clear that pill-taking was among the most dominant factors in their lives. We used that information to establish a bond.

In order to find out how people decide which brand of booze to drink, we built a Liquor Adoption Model. What we learned was pretty interesting.

At the very top of the alcohol pyramid in every market, we found, is a tiny group of people we called Creators. These are the most upscale restaurateurs and celebrities. Madonna is a Creator. People who truly create trends out of nothing. Whether they are consciously determining culture or simply acting on individual instincts and whim, what they do counts.

Around them sits a group we termed Disciples, acolytes who learn the latest trends from the Creators and care deeply about the aesthetics of the products they use, how things look. These people are extremely hip but not very social.

Around them are the Believers, trend followers who are every bit as social as the Disciples are not, who bring the Disciples together with a select group of the initiated. Believers have a huge role in the manufacture of trends. They are the people who spread the word. The initiated pass that word to the public.

The outer ring, who hear of these trends now fourth-hand, is the Mass. Trends, and brands, get adopted outward. Absolut, for instance, was among the first of the cool super-premium vodkas. Initially it was marketed by hipster bartenders and gays, then the trend watchers got involved, and finally it became the brand people asked for when they wanted some aura of chic. After that, other super-premium brands moved into the inner circles.

When we sent anthropologists to talk to both Disciples and Believers, we found some fine stuff. A large proportion of Disciples, the antisocial crew, had no siblings; they were only children. We found that fascinating. Was it the solitary nature of their childhood, the necessity of playing by themselves, that allowed them to collect and appreciate unusual ideas? They tended to be high achievers and they art-directed their lives. They art-directed their names on the mailboxes in their apartment buildings; they would spend twenty minutes talking about which coffeepot they'd bought; they subscribed to magazines you've never heard of. These folks weren't all gay, just very into their world and how it looked.

Disciples would never spread a trend. They'd be perfectly happy sitting in their perfect environment enjoying their new-found toys in their own surroundings. It was the Believers, who were their friends, who created the social setting, invited the Disciples out, and connected them to other people. These other people brought it to the outside world.

We became believers.

When we were working on Tanqueray gin, we didn't hold focus groups in our regular facilities; we held them in bars. We recruited people to come not to focus groups but to little parties. And because these gatherings were in licensed premises, we were allowed to serve alcohol. People arrived dressed for the occasion, the mood was right, our interviewees could taste other drinks, and the discussion got looser as the evening went on. As a result, our information had more substance. Standing at a bar, drink in hand, people were more honest about how they felt on a date and why they chose certain brands. This was valuable information we might not have gotten in the one-way-mirror setting of a focus group conference room.

Ikea was a Deutsch client for twelve years. We launched the brand in this country and by the year 2000 they had the highest advertising awareness of any furniture retailer in their market. Our campaign for the previous three years had been all about life stages. We showed a family moving, a couple adopting a baby, a couple trying to have a baby, a couple building a house on a lake for their retirement home, and about twenty other life scenarios. Every major life event had been illustrated in the advertising, and that's the way people thought about Ikea. If they moved, if their kid went to college, if they had a baby—people came running to Ikea. "It's a big country, someone's got to furnish it."

It worked. Everyone who was ever going to come to an Ikea had been there at least once. Ikea growth was maxed out.

But we still had to increase sales. How? The company wasn't opening many new stores or breaking into new markets. Obviously, we had to get people to come back more often. We had to get them to come in and shop when there wasn't a huge life-change going on.

We surveyed and found families who had been to Ikea only once, for one of those major events. Then we sent Deutsch account planners into selected homes. Sometimes our researchers even stayed overnight so they could really get into family life.

What did they find? That people live with stuff that's not great. You just get used to it. Look in the living room. The rug is a little worn, but it got worn slowly; you don't really notice that you need a new rug. If your four-year-old spills grape juice on it, *then* you realize that not only is there the juice stain but, you know, it's really ragged on the edges where the kids have been running. The dog peed on it once, too.

Look in the kitchen. Especially if you've got kids, stuff breaks. After a short while the glasses don't match. You don't think much of it. But when you've invited your sorority sisters over and have to put out refreshments, *then* you look in the cabinet and say, "Oh my God, I don't have six glasses that are the same in this entire house."

You've gotten used to the mess. It takes an emotionally charged event to get you to see how shabby some things have become. Then you suddenly have the need for a new rug or a set of glassware, the kinds of things Ikea provides in volume. We called these little mini-crises "Daily Disasters."

We came back and wrapped the whole next campaign around this idea. We created a series of very charming fifteen-second spots. One was called "Paperboys":

Three young paperboys are standing on a street corner, straddling their bikes. It's clearly chilly. Early morning. They're looking up at a window. You see a clock. It turns 6:00 am. You hear the alarm buzz. A woman's hand hits the "Off" button. Half-naked, the woman stands up and stretches. Right by the window. Cut to the paperboys looking up. Their faces are filled with amazement. A title card comes on-screen.

"Curtains?"

"Starting at $12."

Everyone understands immediately.

Another was called "Typo":

A guy is getting ready to send out résumés. Hundreds of them are stacked neatly next to his printer. A stack of envelopes sits beside them. The man's wife walks by, picks up a letter from the top of this gigantic pile, and starts reading.

"Dear Sir or Madman . . ."

He's spelled it wrong five hundred times. The title card comes up:
"Wastebaskets . . . and everything else you need for your home office."
And the price. It's low.

The campaign drove a lot of traffic, solved a huge business problem, and ran for many years.

These days you can go to any drugstore and buy a wastebasket; the way to get people to buy one at Ikea was to pull the emotional trigger and connect with that mini-crisis. And we probably wouldn't have found that trigger if we hadn't spent time getting to the emotional element in people's homes. Would not have gotten there.

When a subject is very intimate, we'll hire a psychologist to do the interviews (with box of Kleenex handy). That gives us a great insight into people's value systems and why they do what they do. We use psychologists frequently in pharmaceutical research because people will tell them things they might not tell a stranger around a conference table.

We pitched Tylenol. Tylenol competes in the crowded arena of over-the-counter pain relievers. This is an old category and all the brands in it have almost become commodities. Well, as we looked into the future we found the world was very much about wellness, but also about managing the risks that are growing all around us. People were increasingly concerned about and interested in taking care of themselves. That's no secret. So when we brought Tylenol to a new place in the market, we didn't use the words "pain relief"; our positioning was: Tylenol—The Brand That Does Right by You.

With this as our ethos we focused on ways in which Tylenol is unique and then did very brave and very human advertising. Our Tylenol campaign was out there warning you about stomach damage that came from other pain relievers *that you couldn't even feel.* It was out there telling you to read the label and take Tylenol properly or not at all. It was out there showing you that the brand understands the everyday situations that cause you pain.

In print we chose recognizable moments in people's lives and connected them to the brand.

A room filled row after row with injection-molded plastic chairs, the kind you see in airports, the kind you can just never get comfortable in.

And the line: "You're going to a three-day symposium and your backache is coming along."

A marathon runner, shot from the waist down, wrapped in post-race aluminum foil, holding a trophy.

"Endorphins don't last."

A darkened stand-alone house at night. All the lights out except one, burning the midnight oil.

"Bills, bills, bills."

And with each of them, the tag line: "Stop. Think. Tylenol."

We acted like the buddy who would always do right by you.

We expanded Tylenol's consumer base by seeing where the world was moving, seeing what the brand was, and bringing those worlds together. Our campaign was less about the product's benefits than it was about its value system, its religion. That is what we're constantly trying to do. Then the question becomes, How do you bring that to life in a creative form?

We created a fifteen-second spot for Mitchum deodorant, a Revlon product. It's an antiperspirant, it works great, but we needed to find a way to attract attention using less money than the other players. The category is full of guys sweating from sports or nerves and guys having fabulous women fall all over them because they use the right brand. We did something very different.

A guy hails a yellow cab. You know by the bustle of the street that it's New York City. He gets in and one second later the driver jumps out. The consumer gets that New York cabdrivers are known to smell awful, and if even a cabbie can't take this guy, he must really need a better deodorant. We feel his pain.

It's a funny scene and we can laugh at it. Okay, says the consumer, I'll buy your antiperspirant. All those products work pretty good, but you and I really see eye to eye about much more than that.

When all is said and done, that is what makes great advertising.

Sometimes you get it wrong. McDonald's, for instance. They introduced a very high visibility campaign called "I'm Lovin' It." Justin Timberlake, his music, thirty seconds of exquisitely hip vignettes, almost to the point where every one of them is a cliché: a father and his baby, both with Mohawks; skateboarders; storefront break-dancers. Super-groovy. Looks like it's sliced right out of MTV. Clearly they did research and found that where Mickey D's had once had some street cred, McDonald's was no longer relevant, people didn't think it was cool, and its consumer base wasn't getting any younger.

Well, they got the research right, but at first I thought they missed on the DNA of the brand. While McDonald's does need younger customers, hipness isn't critical. McDonald's is golden arches, it's families, it's Middle America. The new ads are desperately trying to be relevant and hip—they're rap, they're white, they're black—and they ring false. McDonald's was trying to drape themselves in some kind of currency, but it just wasn't who they are. You look at the spots and say, "I don't know if that's black advertising or white advertising or what it is. It's young advertising." It's a young voice and it's presented well, so it's a credible young voice. But I thought it was speaking for the wrong brand.

The smarter move, I thought, would have been to somehow flip where the convention is going and say, "You know what? The new cool is here. Families is the new cool. Reverence is the new irreverence." Turn the worlds upside down. You need to bring those two worlds together either by turning a convention inside out and making it work for you or by making your product work toward that convention. It is the intersection that is important. On that campaign, I thought, McDonald's missed. Turns out I was wrong; it was a tremendously successful campaign.

McDonald's did finally move in the right direction. The real solution for them was when they recognized that the problem was in the product itself—the relentless reliance on the hamburger in a time of increasing health consciousness—and added salads to their menu. With that alteration of the product but not the ethos, they were back on track.

There was a TV ad for the Hummer that I thought was wonderful. A bunch of kids are racing homemade go-karts. Very retro, harking back to the simple days of a long-gone childhood. All the riders in their slick mini–Formula Ones are hightailing it down a hill, but this one preteen in his clunky-looking handmade version of a Hummer doesn't follow the race course. He's the only one out there with such a unique machine. The kid cuts his own way through the great outdoors, blazes his own trail, and to everyone's surprise glides past the finish line in first place and wins the race. All to the accompaniment of the Who's "Happy Jack," a song about a boy who goes his own way:

But they couldn't stop Jack, or the waters lapping
And they couldn't prevent Jack from feeling happy.

What a wonderful spot. It's just a simple truth, understanding what that brand is all about. Hummers, they're telling you, are for people who want to go against convention, who want to show that they like to ride the rockier road. They pride themselves on having a bigger and better machine and they're very pleased to be outsmarting and outdoing all the Yuppies around them. The Who track attracts its older target audience by implicitly saying this is for my "*g-g-g*eneration": We're talking to you! It's a marvelous intersection of what the product does deliver—a big, cool-looking machine—and its attitude: "I can find a shortcut. It may be bumpier but it's exciting and I'm a winner." That is the Hummer attitude about life and it's very appealing.

Nike is among the most brilliant brands. Nike is the ultimate mass brand, yet it has a strong antiestablishment intelligence and it continues to position itself as nonconformist and extraordinary. When people buy into the Nike ethos, they're looking to be out of the ordinary. The actual positioning is something like Authentic Sport. They're saying, "If I put these sneakers on, I'm about pure athleticism. I'm about doing my best. I'm about individualism. I'm about pushing myself hard. I'm about being an individual in this do-the-best-I-can world."

At the end of the day I think we all want to think of ourselves as extraordinary. Some people live it, some don't. But ask anybody if they're ordinary. "Are you ordinary?" "No." Nobody thinks they're ordinary. Or at least in their dreams they're not ordinary. "Do you think you're typical?" Of course not. Who thinks she's typical? We're not looking for typical. We're looking for universally individual. *Just do it!* The best campaigns take the individual and unite him with all the people who think his special way.

In the world of advertising, the consumer votes for a company with his wallet. The company presents its ethos and the customer says, *I bond to what you stand for*—or, *I don't. I like the way you think; I think the same way, you're the beer/furniture/airline/sneaker/truck/movie/antiperspirant for me.* How can you tell? Sales.

A person, a brand, a country—the dynamic is no different. The United States is a brand. It's a set of values. Right now we're not selling our brand internationally very well because we're seen as being more about imperialism and power at all costs than about maintaining peace or bringing prosperity and hope. We need to present ourselves with more heart and less hubris. What is the United States? Our icon, our logo, is the Statue of Liberty. It is a beautiful graphic statement that the United States is about freedom and independence and democracy. We shouldn't be that hard a sell.

Presidents are sold as brands. There's a famous quote from

John F. Kennedy's father, Joe Kennedy: "We're going to sell Jack like soap flakes." President Kennedy was about optimism; that was his brand. JFK was the physical embodiment of a war-tested generation coming forward saying: "There can be a new age. We can be better." *The New Frontier.* But we would have to work for it. *"Ask not what your country can do for you; ask what you can do for your country"* is one of the greatest, most effective advertising lines in history. The Peace Corps and VISTA were a direct result. It's ironic that the Kennedy family was among the wealthiest in the country at the time and JFK himself had had every advantage, yet he was seen as representing the Everyman hope of a whole nation.

Richard Nixon's brand, on the other hand, always had a negativity attached to it. Though he came from lower-middle-class stock, he was carrying the flag for the establishment, and his voice and physical appearance synced up with his untrustworthiness. It was only when, in 1968, his advisers came up with a brand they called "the New Nixon" that he was able to distance himself from that negativity and win. Of course, this points up the power of advertising. Richard Nixon's view of the world was not new; he'd simply been rebranded.

And as with so many promises, that redefinition fell short. Nixon left office in disgrace. Sooner or later the product has to produce; over time, no amount of advertising can sell a bad product.

It can sell a good one. We've created a brand in Deutsch Inc. that has a real ethos to it. Deutsch is about aggressiveness; it's about turning convention upside down; it's about winning. Winning is the only thing. Failure is not an option. It's about contemporariness; it's about smarts. There is a value system to this place. I believe that at its core, no matter how big we get, Deutsch is the Little Engine That Could. That sense of ourselves as the little guys pervades everything we do. And while we don't advertise to attract clients, our agency, our people, and our entire body of work serves the same function.

At Deutsch we teach our people to think in the bigger arena, to look for the client's larger ethos, to find that place for the brand to live that is larger than the sum of its parts, the place that intersects where the world is going and where their business can go. That's more than good advertising, that's good business.

The Corporate Homeland Security Theory

I gave our architect three words: industrial art gallery.

Its physical environment can say a lot about how an organization sees itself. It's your home. Live in it.

In 1999 we outgrew our offices on Park Avenue South and went looking for space. I was never going to inconvenience our staff or clients by moving to a part of town that was inefficient. Moving out of town was out of the question; even if it had been cheaper to move to New Jersey, it would have been the wrong statement. Because we were innovators, trailblazers, on the cutting edge yet ruled by common sense, we weren't ever going to move to Midtown and become a Madison Avenue firm. That wasn't going to happen. I wanted a part of town that was new but not yet super hot, one that our presence could make even hotter, a place where we could get a great deal because that area or that building would be elevated by our presence. I wanted a very open space because we ran a very open operation.

I found an entire floor, 120,000 square feet, in a building downtown in Manhattan's meat-packing district. The space ran from Fifteenth to Sixteenth Street, from Eighth to Ninth Avenue. A wide-open city block, east to west and north to south. You can sense a real estate wave as it starts to move and the area just had the whiff of excitement. It has since become the hottest area in Manhattan. The building's owners had nothing but back-office tenants and were looking for a front-office name to make their mark. I always want to be in the new frontier; I don't want to pay for someone else's pioneering. The guy after me paid that price after we had credentialed the place.

It was the old Port Authority building. They used to drive trucks right inside. The floors were old and beat-up, but they were original concrete, not some newly poured facsimile. There was an aura of authenticity to the entire space that was unassailable.

I found a brilliant architect, Fred Schwartz, whose portfolio was impeccable and seemed to have the taste level I was looking for: simple, raw but sophisticated. I met him and liked his attitude and found he was at that position in his career arc where he could build his brand further by putting his soul into our place. (Apparently it worked. Several years later, after the tragedy of 9/11, Fred was runner-up for the redesign of the World Trade Center. Actually, he won the competition but got undermined by politics.)

I didn't give Fred a set of pictures cut out of architectural magazines; that would have defeated his imagination. I gave him three words: industrial art gallery. In a gallery there is nothing but the paintings, and I wanted a simplicity and starkness that would suggest that the advertising we placed on our walls was highly valued. I wanted our people and the work we produced to be the things of value, but I wanted a very industrial feel. I wanted to make the statement to clients that this place is very utilitarian, very lunch-pail—we were doing business, after all—but very cutting-edge, because that is the best of both worlds. I wanted the client to look around and say: "I've got hard worker bees here. There are no frills, yet I'm far forward." I wanted, in effect, a factory producing art.

There was nothing in his portfolio of this scale, yet the architect clearly understood the vision. We were very Less is More; there's a rawness to us, there's an incredible respect for people and for communication through people; we're tough in certain ways—there is concrete on the floor, it's a hard place—yet everybody, no matter whether they sit in a cube in the middle of the floor or in an office with a huge window with vast city views and a glass door, sees outward. That's who we are and that's the way we do things; that's what we believe: open, transparent, communicating.

In designing 120,000 square feet, there was not one material, not one piece of furniture that Fred brought in or suggested that I rejected out of hand. He got it. He understood what we were about as a company. His placement of offices was magnificent. Most companies segregate the media department, the creative department, the account teams. I wanted cross-pollination; I wanted to force our people to get out of a three-office department suite and walk across a quarter of the place to meet with their colleagues, and to get a full view of the company while they were doing it.

I purposely placed my office at the farthest end from the entrance so I would be forced to walk through the entire company every day. I was going to get a full view and a complete sense of the buzz of the place every time I came in. The partners' offices, mine included, were nice but not the opulent spaces that were common in other agencies.

The space is fun. You want people to want to stay, to feel that this is their community. We've got a balcony overlooking downtown Manhattan that makes eating lunch here a pleasure. Sun streams in all day long, except when it's raining or sleeting or snowing, when you get the most amazing weather shows. People are accessible to each other; the doors are all glass; there are no secret hideaways.

Clients are blown away by it. Even for the most conservative clients, the bankers and such, the day at the agency is kind of like a day cheating on their wife; they're out, they don't have to answer to anyone, it's fun. If they arrive at an office and see something that feels exactly like the one they just left, well, they figure, "What are we hiring these people for? We can do that." But these businesspeople, even if they're in a very conservative, wood-panel business, can see the intelligence, sophistication, and cutting-edge quality of our place. They've never seen anything like it.

The sheer size of the floor knocks them out. It's a city block! They crane their necks up at the exposed ventilation pipes, several feet in diameter, that run the length of the building and say, "Well, I see you certainly didn't waste any money on extras." They like that; they figure the money is going toward their work instead. (It's ironic, because it was considerably more expensive to restore the factory-like feel than it would have been to hide it all behind a dropped ceiling.)

But they see the crisp white cubes in the work areas and understand that there is sophistication but no frills around here. Exactly what you want a client to think about your business! As I have already described the agency to them: "It's about the people. These guys work like animals; they're very sophisticated and clear in their thinking." It's all there and you can see the clients taking it in.

I can wear jeans and a T-shirt in this place because I have this great air cover around me. Even if the client doesn't appreciate my casual attire, there is obviously a lot of weight and depth and gravitas to the office itself, which speaks to the weight, depth, and gravitas of our work.

The office architecture is smart. Even in its unconventionality, it's smart. In its functionality, in the classic nature of its design, it's smart. As with any great architecture, the offices look contemporary but are, in fact, timeless. The space will feel great ten years from now, an eternity if you're trying to be cutting-edge. The lines are simple; the colors are not of-the-moment and therefore soon to be out-of-date: they're basic gray and white.

And of course, the work on the walls and the work on the reels is equally smart, which is the point.

Analyzing Advertising's Corporate Inferiority Complex

I go to industry functions and sniff the other baboons. I smell fear.

Ad guys? Hucksters, schlockmeisters, toadies, goofballs. That's what you see in the movies; it's how we're portrayed on TV. The buffoonery of Darren Stevens on *Bewitched*. The fear of Michael and Elliot on *thirtysomething*. The slick chauvinism of the Mel Gibson character in *What Women Want*. Very subservient, always in a jam. I can't think of any media example in which an advertising executive is shown as self-actualized or super-professional. In the public's mind we're either smooth, amoral bastards who will say anything to get you to buy whatever piece of crap we happen to be selling at the moment or we're those bumbling guys who will do anything to make their client happy.

How wrong are they?

We see the same movies, we watch the same TV. The images have become a self-perpetuating image in our own eyes. In real life, ad guys may wear slick suits but they often look beaten up, afraid of their own shadows. They don't seem to be in charge; they have a submissive mentality, as if they're all waiting to be fired.

Bankers, lawyers, accountants, consultants, and advertising executives are all in the service business. Yet only we in advertising are held in such low regard by both the public and the clients we serve. Bankers, lawyers, accountants, and consultants are not called upon to perform the extra toady things we are. They're supposed to build a client's business; we're supposed to perform personal services. And we, as an industry, do. We shouldn't, and at Deutsch we try very hard not to.

If I have an investment banker who sends me an extravagant gift for Christmas, who is always trying to take me places and curry my favor, maybe he's not that good! The best people don't bow and scrape. It's not that they're arrogant; they provide a service for you and don't feel compelled to put cookies on top. If I have a vendor who is trying too hard, beyond the service he's supposed to be giving me, I wonder why.

In advertising, client loyalty is to the bottom line, not to the supplier. And at core I think most advertising executives don't believe they have a differentiated product that is superior to their competitors'. They feel they can be shot at any time. It's an anxious world.

It doesn't have to be. I learned an extremely valuable lesson from Howard Rubenstein, one of the top public relations executives in the country. Early in my time at David Deutsch Associates we had hired his firm, and because we were having some financial problems, we were about sixty days late with our payment. Howard called and said, "Donny, I see that you guys are two months back. Just understand, this is unacceptable for us. We need to be paid on the first of the month, and if that is a problem, we are not going to do business together."

Other companies might have been concerned about losing

our business and let us slide. But what Rubenstein showed me was that he valued his service. He wasn't shy about demanding to be paid because he knew he was providing a quality product at the right price. From that moment on I knew I would never lose the respect of a client by asking to be paid promptly. If I allow a client to pay late, what am I really saying? One, that I am not as good as my word; and two, maybe what I am providing to the client is not as good as I say it is. If you don't value it, how will they? The same holds true for offering to cut one's price. How valuable is your product if you're willing to discount its value?

Howard taught me all that in one well-delivered message. He did it nicely, but I got the idea strongly. I walked right back to my accounting department and said, "Make sure we get that out today."

Anyone selling a commodity can be replaced. The buyer can find it down the street better, cheaper, packaged more seductively, and you're gone. Desperation is rampant in our industry. It's not the exception, it's the rule. Everything is tenuous because so many people don't truly value what they bring to the table. Clients reinforce this by making agencies into interchangeable parts, hiring and firing them on whim and at will. When you do not have faith in your unique gifts, you will do anything to keep a job.

Many agencies train their people to think, "Whatever the client wants. Just make him happy." It's amazing to me. We are trained professionals with considerable expertise, but when we're faced with even the hint of reservation, we roll over like dogs. We're in a service business and we service our clients out the ass. The amount of crap we feel we have to do—and we do!—is outrageous.

And it's not like I haven't done it. I did it for years. Lawyers don't do this kind of stuff for their clients. Accountants, financial advisers, they don't soil themselves to keep business. Ad people are pimps and stooges. There's nothing you can't invite us all to do that we won't do. The operative concept is, "whatever it takes."

When I was working for my father we had a client, Nicholas

Laboratories, that manufactured black skin tone cream. The CEO was a pleasant Australian who had just moved to America with his family, worked in New York, and had settled in suburban New Jersey. I was young, maybe twenty-three, and he had a daughter who was graduating from high school. She was a delightful girl; she didn't know a lot of people; she didn't have a date to the prom. The CEO asked my dad whether I would take her. It was fun, it was charming. But putting aside for a moment the fact that he really didn't want me anywhere near his teenage daughter, what could possess a man to ask a business associate to escort his daughter?

Do things change? Twenty years later the two head guys at my Los Angeles office were invited by the president of Mitsubishi to attend his daughter's high school graduation party at their house in Orange County. A hundred teenagers. Of course they went.

The stuff we put up with.

When we were in the throes of servicing Ikea, a huge account for us, a new president of Ikea Canada came onboard and wanted to get to know me. Ikea is a kumbaya company, they make every effort to be personable, and the new executive insisted that I fly up to Canada, somewhere outside of Toronto, to have dinner with him and his family. "You should come up. You'll stay over." I flew in, we had dinner, we talked, we had a couple of drinks, we went back to his home, and it came time for me to go to sleep. "Here, Donny." I found myself in the basement in the freezing cold in a racing-car trundle bed with Speed Racer sheets thinking, "What the fuck am I doing?" The indignities we allow. It's such a service business.

But as Deutsch has developed, as our need for individual clients has decreased, I've made a true effort to stick my chest out and be proud of what I do, be proud of my agency, be proud of my industry, and treat clients as equals rather than enter into a submissive, subservient role.

There is a boilerplate for calculating agency fees throughout the advertising industry. It used to be media commissions, but that wasn't fair to either side; if a client had a windfall increase in spending, that didn't mean the agency had done proportionally more work; conversely, if the client cut the budget at the end of the year after all the work had been done, the agency was left out in the cold. Business changed, and for the past several decades agencies have totaled the direct salary of staff working on the business, factored in overhead, added a profit of fifteen to twenty percent, and come up with a figure.

Within the past few years, however, a new concept has been pushed forward by the clients. They have developed procurement divisions in their companies that come to us and say, "I want to see how much your overhead is. I want to examine your salaries; I want to analyze your rent." They have begun a wholesale system of micromanagement of the agencies' internal workings.

Can you imagine what would happen if I called Goldman Sachs, which charges me certain fees for managing my money, or Simpson Thatcher, which does my legal work, and said, "Before I pay your retainer, I want to know your partners' direct salaries, I want to know the rent you pay on your offices, I want to know your people's travel-and-entertainment expenses"? It's unfathomable! What industry rolls over and does that?

Advertising.

The agencies caved. Rather than risk losing the business, they gave in to the clients' demands and provided extensive details of their economics. With this information the clients began to squeeze agencies' margins to the point where they couldn't supply good service anymore, and many simply couldn't succeed. Cut to the bone, their margins shrunk, their work suffered, and whatever profits the agencies might have been making were slashed deeply.

Pfizer Pharmaceuticals was one of our major clients. They paid us close to $17 million in annual fees, which was approximately eight percent of our business. We had had their account for nearly four years, we had built Zoloft and Zyrtec into billion-dollar blockbuster drugs, and when it came time to negotiate a new contract, they demanded our information. They sat in a meeting, pointed to the blue logo on their business card, and said, "We do not deny that you put billions of dollars on the board for what you've done. Having said that, our procurement people would like to know your rent on the fourteenth floor."

That was absurd. By that formula, because I was running a lean business and had negotiated an excellent lease, they would pay me less than they would to some fat-cat schmuck uptown who was being gouged. They were going to pay me less because I was the pioneer who moved downtown first?

I told them, "If you have an issue with the fees we charge, let us know. We'll work backward, we'll scale back the services we provide. But I'm running my business; you're not running it. How much my people make is none of your business. How much our rent is is none of your business. What Val DiFebo pays for a cab ride home is none of your business."

(Interestingly, when the government had gone to the pharmaceutical industry and wanted to get into its pricing, pharmaceuticals said that was confidential and proprietary to their business model.)

Pfizer had outside cost consultants on their payroll and I knew as soon as those guys saw our figures they'd call up every one of our other clients and say, "Hey, I just got into Deutsch's bowels and I can figure out how to save you a ton of money." We were operating on high margins when everyone else in the industry was operating on single digits and going out of business and couldn't figure out why. Why? Because they were putting guns to their own heads.

This didn't take vision. The other agencies were acting out of complete idiocy, complete fear and panic; it was a self-fulfilling prophecy for failure. We had and still have a business model that was hugely successful—and equally important, successful for our clients. We find the best people, we pay them a premium, they put in extremely long hours, and one week of their work is equal in quality to two weeks of anybody else's. Clients don't understand that. They tell us "You're thirty percent above the norms." We say, "Yeah, but we don't work only eighty hours a week. I can go and hire twice as many people, who will cost you forty percent more than you're paying now, and I'll have a mediocre organization. Is that what you'd like me to do?" In fact, it is; they'd be happier with that old model because it's one they understand. They're complete sheep.

Pfizer insisted. They demanded our information. I refused. We had created for them the most successful advertising ever done in the pharmaceutical category; we had built their brands; now they were going to bargain with us over our profits? Forget about it.

They weren't budging.

I had to walk away from the account.

We left $17 million in revenue on the table, but I really had no choice; I did what was right for our business. Pfizer did what it felt was right for its business. We filled Pfizer's slot with Johnson & Johnson and significantly expanded our relationship with Novartis. Pfizer found another agency; someone else capitulated, opened up their books, opened up their veins, and signed their contract. Pfizer probably negotiated a better profit margin, but they didn't get the benefit of our work. Good luck to them.

Solving the Creative-Commercial Equation

The care and feeding of creatives. How to get great work in service of the bottom line.

Most people who work for a living are motivated first and foremost by money. Obviously they want to feel good about themselves and all that fuzzy stuff, but most people work for a paycheck. Creative people—"creatives," we call them in the advertising trade, but I'm talking about all creative people, whether they're screenwriters, designers, commercial producers, musicians—are completely different. Money matters, but more than anything, creatives are motivated by producing work that is an extension of themselves and that other creative people will aspire to. If you're going to work with them, you need to understand that fact.

I've never met another group of people to whom peer-set approval means more than the outside world's, more than their boss's, sometimes even more than their own. I don't know for certain whether this exists in all creative businesses or only in our field, but it is vitally important to advertising creatives that the other fifteen thousand people in the advertising creative community think what they do is good. That club is very important to them. If they have an ad on TV that the public loves, that their boss loves, but that other creatives think sucks, they are devastated.

Creatives are not seeing the world like most people. They're zealots. To a creative, compromise is defeat; to change an element in any way that they feel compromises their arts-and-crafts project is a failure. My job in motivating these people is to somehow let them meet their agenda, but not at the cost of what is really necessary, which is to produce advertising that sells the product. When it's done right, both worlds come together.

If you're a champion of pure creative work at the expense of everything else, you'll end up with a very small business, whether it's an advertising boutique, a clothing store, a publishing company, a record label. If that's what you want, fine, but you won't be getting a lot of work, and as a result, ironically, you won't be getting the best creative opportunities. Over the years I have tried to deconstruct that mind-set, to train creatives to think beyond their cohorts. "Fuck the creative awards and fuck what other creatives think," I'll tell them. "The G-spot is making your mother love it, making me love it." I still want them to do great work, but I need them to understand my definition of great work: exciting creative that moves product. ("Creative" is an ad industry term of art for creative work product.)

And I pay attention. You tend to get smarter, better work that way. If creative people feel that you care about their project, the toy that they're building—that it matters to you, though not at the expense of the bottom line—that's all they care about. More than money.

More than fucking money!

I've never cared about award shows, I'm not playing for that prize, so I've always been an outcast in the creative community.

Number one, award shows are judged by a lot of people I wouldn't hire, many of whom are recycled creatives. People who have the time to judge award shows have entirely too much time on their hands; why aren't they working? Number two, much award-winning advertising tends to look the same: the highly intellectual concept, the pithy headline. It outsmarts itself. Our Mitsubishi campaign, with people moving in odd ways and singing in their cars, would never win any awards—it's just great advertising. People love it. The elite creative community might look down on it. "Where is the idea? Where is the deep pocket of intellectual capital that challenges the mind? It's just people singing in their cars." Yeah. That's the brilliance of it. It is advertising that people love and that motivates them to feel great about a product they didn't feel great about before.

And for the most part, clients don't care about your statuettes, and I don't think they should. Early in my career I was in a new-business pitch and, in discussing our credentials, mentioned that just a week earlier our Ikea campaign had won a Gold Lion at the Cannes Advertising Festival. I saw the client's head tilt. The look on his face told me, "What, do you think I care about that? And if *you* care about that, your head's in the wrong place, pal." A great creative reputation is a necessity in our business, but to me, great creative speaks for itself and you don't need awards to tell you what's first-rate.

This is not a universally held opinion. I recently met the chairman and CEO of a huge global advertising network. I asked him how he spent his time. He told me, "Well, I travel around the world making sure our creative offices are all producing great work. Do you know that ten of our top fifteen offices are number one . . ." and he gave me the name of some report that told him so. I'd never heard of it. "Oh," he said, "they track which agencies win the most awards."

I couldn't believe this CEO was grading his agency on such

foolish criteria. Some tracking agency! I said to myself, though not to him, "That's what I would expect from a twenty-three-year-old. What world are you in?"

The agencies that focus on awards are trying to credential themselves. Nonsense. Let's compare results; how has your award-winner rewarded your client? That's the bottom line. The awards mean nothing.

Except to the creatives. From their point of view, it's how they make their reputations, how they ascend in their crowd, and how they get better jobs. So maybe I was a little overzealous when I told them, "Fuck creative awards." Of course I don't subscribe to the theory that the more creative an ad is the less it will sell. As far as I'm concerned, creativity that doesn't sell is not creative. I believe that if you have your eye on the ball, and you understand going in the supposition that you are trying to move product, then making your advertising fresher and more innovative will usually be a big plus.

I was having a conversation recently about the 2003 Super Bowl ads. The woman I was talking with said, "You know what commercials I love? The *'Whassup?'* commercials." I asked, "What beer was it for?" Now, granted, she wasn't in the target audience, but she couldn't come up with the product. I love those ads, too; they have great DNA saying to guys, "We get you"; but if there wasn't enough branding in them, they're a failure. At the end of the day, if you're talking about the *"Whassup?"* spot and not the *"Whassup?"* Budweiser spot, what's up?

Will we screen a creatively advanced commercial and have the client say, "Can we have more car footage in it?" or "We need more time on the logo"? Sure, that happens all the time. And if, for some reason, the ad in its current form isn't whetting people's appetites and celebrating the product sufficiently, sometimes you do need more car in there. I will never say, "Oh, don't do that, it makes the ad less creative." On the flip side, if the ad makes the car look great and the client is saying, "I think there should be five more seconds of car," which would weaken the ad's emotional connection *and ultimately cost the client sales,* I will push back. That's what I get paid for, my ability to look at an ad and say, "This is going to work." Ultimately, that's what the craft is.

That's the perspective I try to teach creatives: innovative work in service of the bottom line. Some creatives get it, but not enough.

Some agencies treat creatives as if they're a different species. They have nicer offices than the account executives; they must have certain kinds of Evian water in these offices and when they travel; you can't argue with them. They're invested with a certain star quality. They're prima donnas. Divas.

Bullshit.

I'm a believer in true democracy and I have no patience with this sort of posturing. Creatives have a unique skill, as do media planners, as do account executives. There are good ones and bad ones. At Deutsch we de-diva-ize everyone.

I understand that there are certain cultural differences. I wouldn't ask a creative to punch a clock at nine in the morning; that would be counterproductive. But I am as blunt with them as I am with anyone; my vocabulary doesn't change from office to office. I wouldn't tell anyone, "That's a piece of shit"; that would be cruel, destructive, and stupid. I do hear stories about creative directors who won't even look at creatives while they're presenting, who throw storyboards on the ground and stomp on them, saying, "I wouldn't give that to my cat to shit on!" That's just a power game. There's no point in being a bully.

I believe in candor and I choose my words carefully. "That sucks" doesn't move the work forward. I prefer to say, "I think you missed and here is why." I don't pull punches, but I try to get my points across constructively, with directness and honesty, without derision or sarcasm. "I don't want you turning down that path. I understand you put a lot of effort into it, and I see why you went there, but I've got to tell you . . ."

It All Comes Back to Babes

(Or studs, depending on your orientation.)
You've heard the phrase "Sex sells." As if we're supposed to apologize for it. Never. In fact we should celebrate it.

Sex in advertising? I'll put it another way. When does advertising intelligently portray intimacy?

Advertising is a mirror to society. It has to be in order to connect and sell. To be most effective, advertising needs to be in touch with up-to-date sexual and romantic mores. In the '60s, when free love and the pill were all the rage, ads showed girls draped on the hoods of cars; "The Stripper" sold shaving cream; Joe Namath, the embodiment of happy sexuality, was an advertising icon.

The first couple is our royalty and during most administrations they set the tone for the entire country. In the '70s when Jimmy Carter lusted in his heart, there was more than enough lust on the ad pages in *Playboy*. In the Reagan era, while sex was proper, you knew in some strange way that Nancy and Ronnie were getting down. Then when the AIDS epidemic broke out and your dick could kill you, advertising switched from sex to romance; raw, sexual ads were replaced by the softer themes. Now that AIDS, while certainly still a tremendous problem, seems to be more under control, more overt sexuality is on the rise. Watch MTV; everything is about sex. You couldn't have put the Coors twins or the Miller Lite bikini mud wrestlers on the air during the AIDS crisis; it would have been inappropriate—and it wouldn't have generated sales.

You weren't sure about Bill and Hillary, but you knew that Bill was getting some; he was a sexy president, as was revealed, and the advertising kept pace. Both the Bushes, 41 and 43, had a neutered sense about them. George the First was actually made manly by rumors of an extramarital affair. Barbara Bush inspired no lust but quite a bit of fear. George W., so little boyish dressed up in his flight suit, doesn't seem to have a sexual bone in his body. He gets on the treadmill and is in bed by nine o'clock. And until they unleashed her during desperate times at the end of the 2004 campaign, Laura Bush appeared to channel Mamie Eisenhower and Lady Bird Johnson and had the pretty veneer and absolute sexlessness of a Stepford Wife. You wonder how that played on the tone and sexuality of the country as a whole.

I believe sex in advertising became less overt and more subdued in the first few years of the millennium because Bush was in the White House and because we came through 9/11, which initially stopped things cold. Recently, however, as terrorism has become a constant concern in our lives, overt sexuality has reappeared and become even more dramatic, because that's where you go for comfort in unsettled times: sex and intimacy. Watch any Armageddon movie; if a couple is together and the world is going to end the following day, of course they have sex.

Today the fashion *is* sex. Girls dress slutty; whether they're sluts or not, that's the look. (This is counterintuitive, since the first couple seems to be having none of it.) As a result, it's hard to find a place you can't use sex to sell anymore.

We've gotten to the point that there was a product on the Super Bowl broadcast that talked about a four-hour erection! It wasn't an ad, it wasn't a copy line, it was a piece of legal disclaimer: If you have a four-hour erection, you should go to a hospital. (I thought, instead of "Go find your doctor," they should have said, "Go find the nearest women's prison.") That was one of the most outrageous, hysterical, over-the-top moments in advertising history. Stopped every male in America in his tracks. And it has lived on in Super Bowl lore. You're sitting there watching the game with your eight-year-old son and he turns to you and asks, "Daddy, what's a 'four-hour erection'?"

There are some areas where selling with sex presents problems. You wouldn't use sex to sell McDonald's; too many kids in the audience. However, in this new world the McDonald's "I'm Lovin' It" campaign is much sexier than anything the chain has ever run and appears to have had a very positive effect on sales. (Obviously driven by their salads; advertising can only do so much.) Packaged goods? No. Household products? Not necessarily; homemakers can be titillated but Mr. Clean is, after all, Mr. *Clean*. Food? Sex is not necessarily the first place you'd go.

Some food, however, crosses over. Coffee and how we drink it—coffee moments—is increasingly a social scene rather than just a beverage. In the '90s, Taster's Choice instant coffee ran a series of ads in which a man and a woman started to percolate and ultimately got pretty hot. This soap opera ad series was quite successful because it didn't appear to be selling coffee—the coffee was incidental to the real action, which may have been moving toward the bedroom—it was selling attraction.

And it sold like crazy; Taster's Choice sales increased by ten percent soon after the ads aired. Unlike what happened with the "*Whassup?*" campaign, people referred to them as the "Taster's Choice ads." Clearly they worked. Folks didn't talk about those ads because they liked a good cup o' joe; they got caught up in an urban seduction and enjoyed the scent of the brew.

But there's no stopping men and women who want to get

laid. We're all putting out scents of who we are, and advertising uses that trail to attract customers. Any product having to do with the external self—fashion, perfume, shampoo, cars—or the social world—cigarettes and lubricants like beer, booze, even soft drinks, which can be social in their own way—is, of course, a prime user.

It's going to be interesting to see how the baby boom generation, the most self-entitled generation ever, deals with its sexuality as it ages. Boomers are still the dominant force in society—we've had back-to-back two-term boomer presidents—and it was a pretty sexy generation to begin with. Mick Jagger is sixty-two and we're not letting him go limp. Most generations have been willing to back off sex at age fifty-five. Not the boomers. No way we're going to back off—and we've got the drugs to prove it. It's no coincidence that, as the sexual revolution generation began aging, Viagra was born.

This society is going to do everything it can to protect its vitality. We're the first generation to feel it has a right to live longer and have more of what it wants for longer periods of time. When previous generations hit their fifties, they began to prepare to sit back and watch as their children took over. This generation wants to keep coming. I think this urgency has tremendous implications, and marketers who can intelligently show aging sexuality are going to hit some real scores.

One of our clients in the late 1980s was Frances Lear, television producer Norman Lear's ex-wife, who was using some of her $100 million divorce settlement to create and launch *Lear's*, a magazine devoted to women of a certain age. I loved Frances very much; she was one of the most inspirational people I've worked for. As has been well documented, Frances was severely bipolar, very dynamic, very bright. The Maude character on TV was based on her. Frances took a real shine to me. I was thirty; she was sixty-five, and she used to hit on me and flirt quite overtly. It was my first experience of what sexual harassment must feel like. I'd walk into a meeting with her and four or five women her age and she'd say, "Look at him. Look at his blue eyes. He exudes sex!" I got a strong taste of what it feels like to be an object, but rather than finding it objectionable, I got a kick out of it.

One winter Sunday, Frances and I were supposed to go to the movies. (Deutsch was a full-service agency.) I arrived at her apartment and she opened the door in an off-the-shoulder sweatshirt. "You know," she said, "it's so cold out, I have a great idea. Instead of going to the movies, I rented a movie. You probably haven't seen it. *The Graduate.*"

I couldn't make this stuff up. Forget that *The Graduate* is my favorite movie of all time. I said, "Frances, we're going to the movies."

She flirted with me all the time but in a very charming, harmless way. Nothing was going to happen, but in my own way I flirted back. It was a business relationship, and part of my job in all business relationships is some form of seduction. If it's with a guy, we might talk football; if an attractive young woman is involved, I might just exude sex. I'll work it. You use what you have.

I'm in shape, I'm decent enough looking, and for a CEO of a large company I'm more dynamic than most. I find that often works to my advantage, but sometimes not. With women it's usually a positive. Also, I usually do well with dynamic top-level guys, but I have found that some mid-level bureaucrats get jealous and give me a hard time. Why? I've made a lot of money, I've got a big company, I do what I want, I say what I want; to someone who's not actualized in his own life that can present a problem, and middle managers have been known to make my life difficult as a result.

We were working to launch *Lear's*, who came to us with a great tag line: "*Lear's:* For the woman who wasn't born yesterday." The target audience was women over forty and our series of ads showed portraits of women in their forties, fifties, and sixties photographed seminude from the waist up in black-and-white, their hands or arms covering their breasts. The photographs were beautifully, tastefully done. They really did show that women are gorgeous, interesting, alluring at any age.

The Sunday *New York Times* wouldn't run them. Why? The clearance guy looked at one of the photos and actually said, "She's older." Then he caught himself. The *Times* was running a truly demeaning ad for Gucci at the time, showing a naked woman and some guy with his foot on her head. That was okay, but a beautiful celebration of older women was somehow over the line. There are ways of pushing things through, however. I said, "I think this is discriminatory and I don't think it'll be very good for you guys if it gets out that you're not accepting ads with women over a certain age." Ultimately the ads did run, and they were among the sexiest ads I've ever done.

But *Lear's* had a problem that it ultimately could not survive: Frances's whole premise was wrong; people did not want to focus on women over forty. Not even the women over forty. Our research showed that older women didn't look in the mirror and see themselves as forty, fifty, or sixty; they saw much younger women. They didn't want to read about the issues, trials, and successes of older women; they wanted to read *Vogue*, see what the twenty-one-year-old models looked like, and see themselves the same way. And if older women weren't interested in older women, who would be? At no time in our history have we been able to sexualize beyond the young. *Lear's* closed in 1993. Frances has since passed away. A great loss.

The Principle of Moral Responsibility and Just Plain Bad Ads

I don't think it's ever good business to offend people, and I don't think there are any great brands that were built on meanness, but the reality is that sometimes you are just going to cross the line.

That's not always a bad thing.

The truly offensive commercials are easy to spot. There was a small, controversial agency in Philadelphia that created a campaign for some youth-oriented downtown clothing store and put Charles Manson in their ad. That's just insensitive and moronic. This is a mass murderer, a guy with a swastika on his head; there's no sane way in the world to celebrate him. I guess the concept was edginess, but that's way over the edge.

The classic bad ad was the guy shooting gerbils out of a cannon and smashing them into a brick wall. Aired during the Super Bowl. Got a lot of attention. But it was bad advertising because (1) it was stupid, offensive, and cruel, and (2) no one remembers the product and there was nothing to define the brand in it. Visit us, we'll kill your pet? This was just a way of saying, "Look how wacky we are."

But the point is not just to be wacky; what you're trying to do is endear your product to the consumer. A pile of dead gerbils won't fill that bill. Can you tell me what company that ad was for and what their product did? Or where they are now? They're out of business. Consumers have a great litmus test. They know when you're just getting attention for attention's sake and they tune out.

I believe, in advertising and in all business, we have a moral responsibility to be honest, to sell within the boundaries of fairness. I don't think there are any great brands built over time that didn't tell the truth. It's no different than one-to-one selling. If I am a peddler and I'm selling you a set of encyclopedias you don't really need, or if I'm selling you a pair of jeans and telling you they look great on you so you'll buy them—I may be playing to your weaknesses, but I don't think there's any moral turpitude in that. Do I think it's wrong to sell aluminum siding under the pretense that it keeps a house fresher or warmer or lasts longer when it really doesn't? Yes, because that is dishonest. Do you need another necktie? No. If I can sell you one and take ten dollars from you and put it in my pocket or my company's, that's capitalism, that's America. Could I ever sell you swampland if I knew it was worthless? No. Could I advertise Zoloft and say, or even hint, that it cures depression when I knew it didn't? No, I couldn't do that.

For the most part, advertising guidelines are on the money— with the exception of one of the most important areas: politics. Political advertising isn't even branded; it is daily communications warfare. The absurdity is that these campaigns play a vital role in selecting the leadership of the country, yet they are scrutinized far less than work selling margarine. With almost no oversight, modern political ads are able to twist and manipulate facts freely.

Why?

A combination of broadcasters' greed—money is coming in and it's coming in fast—and partisan zealotry. The "Swift Boat Veterans" campaign against Senator John Kerry was a low point in

American advertising. The political groups known as 527s have to go; they're a complete backdoor loophole. Both parties do this; in 2004, the Republicans just did it better. We can't have individual interest groups facelessly funding ads; it defeats the whole purpose of honesty and accountability. The network clearance people need to be as vigorous in their inspection of political ads as they are with all others.

However, and this is vital, there's no such thing as network political advertising anymore. The presidential election always comes down to anywhere between seven and fifteen states, and that's where all the money goes: spot television. Ad clearance comes down to the honor and reliability, or lack thereof, of some guys at the local stations. Local stations are invariably looking for ways to make money, and here is all this dough flying in. Will they be scrupulous? What do you think?

What's the solution? I'm not certain. Maybe the networks have to get involved in the local vetting process. On top of that, the country would be well served by a political advertising regulatory system that controlled the flow of money and prevented the spreading of verifiable untruths.

As for the rest of the advertising business, you really can't get on the air and say that a product does something when it doesn't. If anything, the free enterprise system, and fear that your competition will call you on it, keeps you honest. Does that mean that when they shoot an ad for cereal, it doesn't have marbles in the bottom of the bowl to prop up the flakes? No. Does a real-life Whopper ever look like one you see on TV? Does it remotely look like it? No. But is that cheating? We live in a visual world and we assume most people understand there is some beautification of the product going on.

Some of that beautification, however, goes too far. There was a campaign running in New York City on big-time radio stations that promoted a cream that actually claimed women, if they rubbed this product on their breasts, would gain one or two cup sizes. Absurd and amazing. It got clearance.

I have a fundamental problem with a lot of the advertising for high-end cosmetics, where they're selling complete fantasy in a bottle. I'm not a woman, I don't use these products, but when they say, "Put this stuff on and you'll reduce wrinkles and fool nature" . . . it ain't happening, and common sense tells you it ain't happening. Cosmetics marketers could argue, and they do, that if a woman feels better and she thinks she is doing something to help herself, to pamper her skin, to attract attention from whomever she's looking to attract, we're doing her a service by selling her those products. And isn't that what advertising does! It establishes what people want and it sells them their best vision of themselves. That's what marketing is, and it's hard to criticize, it's the fundamental core of business.

But you are setting people up for a fall if what you are telling them is not built on fundamental truths. Pond's and others sell some of their products by calling them age-defying cream. Those words—"age-defying cream"—that's tiptoeing on the precipice. In that phrase is the reason advertising exists. It's a fine line, and right in that little sweet spot is everything that is wonderful and heinous about advertising.

I can take that ad and work back logically and say why it's horrible for women and why it's exquisite.

It's horrible because you are basically saying to a woman, "You have to stay young." Now, one could argue that that sentiment doesn't start with advertising, but we certainly carry it forward. "Your natural beauty, whatever that was, is past. You need to be young. You need to do everything humanly possible, even to the point of disregarding common sense, to stay young because *who you are now is not good.* Whoever you are, you're not good enough."

That's devastating. No one is going to be young forever, and here are millions and millions of dollars being spent to tell women they don't look good. This could cause women to have all kinds of crazy plastic surgeries and have their faces pulled back like they're in a psychic wind tunnel. It could make them feel less good about themselves, make them feel ugly and insecure.

Makes you sick.

That is the obvious "advertising-people-are-scumbag-dickhead-bottom-feeders" line of reasoning. In fact, a woman in San Diego filed a class action lawsuit against Estée Lauder, Neiman Marcus, and Nordstrom for false advertising. "I wasn't getting any younger," she said.

On the other side:

Wait a second. We are giving women, who are feeling increasingly empowered, the opportunity to do everything they can and want for themselves to make themselves feel good. This cream, when a woman goes to sleep, makes her feel she is pampering herself and making herself attractive. It is a gift she gives to herself. And when she uses it, she does feel better about herself, and when she feels better, she looks better. We're giving her this dream. She is getting older and this is one way she can feel younger. And you know what? She may even look in the mirror and, in her mind, look younger. And what is wrong with that?

Women will tell you both of those positions are true. In our research, in focus groups and one-on-one interviews, they will say, "I'm not going to be bullshitted. They can't make me feel bad about myself. I like the way I am now and I don't want to be twenty again." And from the other side of their mouth: "I am getting older and I want to look as good as I can, and I want to feel good, and when I look good, I feel good."

We handled Revlon. Every time someone in our organization tried to create a campaign around the concept "Let's show women as they really are! Let's take photography that is real and not idealized," it got shot down. We showed it to women in focus groups and they said, "I don't like the way that looks. I don't want to see a fashion ad with a forty-six-year-old woman in it, I want to see beautiful women."

Dove ran a campaign in which they showed women as they are, with freckles and minute imperfections. But all the models were still beautiful women! They were celebrating the fact that women look different—"Look, a woman with freckles in a soap commercial!" Big breakthrough—but they were still presenting aspiration by idealizing the image. Show a woman who is not attractive and then we'll be in business.

I'm a health-conscious guy who puts thought into and takes care of his appearance. I get frustrated by men's fitness and health magazines. I look in the mirror and go, "Wow, I'm in great shape for my age! I'm about as good as it's going to get." Then I turn the pages and look at these guys with eight-packs. It's not possible for me to get there, and in a certain way it's demotivating. There is no chance, give up now. I can't work as hard as that guy. Maybe when I was twenty-one I could have, but my body just can't get there anymore. I don't know how that plays out with women, but I know every time I pick up those magazines I get bummed out.

The argument in advertising has always been "the chicken or the egg": Do we make girls anorexic or do anorexic girls use us? A large component of our society's dynamic is based on aesthetic appeal. There has been research done that showed that little children are more drawn to aesthetically attractive other children. The researchers don't know why. At age three, these children haven't yet been bombarded with advertising, so I don't think we create that attraction. Kids simply like attractive children and adults.

A good businessperson ought to be able to arrive at a motivating theme without fakery. There is, however, some insidious marketing being done literally on the streets.

Urban brands are hiring what they call "street teams" to go into ethnic communities, where there is a vital market, and target the underprivileged. This is a big source of both revenue and discomfort in both the liquor and cigarette industries. The marketers make the argument that the underprivileged are also undereducated, not educated enough to make the proper decisions, so these street teams are "helping" them.

I find that whole line of thinking racist and don't believe it for a minute. I think what the companies are preying on is not that the people are uneducated; the poorest person knows that cigarettes are unhealthy. I think they are preying on a culture that is more susceptible to their products because life and health certainly don't have the same premium in a working-class ghetto that they do in a middle-class neighborhood. Not that life is any less precious if you have fewer possessions, but on streets where people are dealing drugs, there's a different code the street teams plug into.

I laughed when they outlawed Joe Camel because the character was encouraging young people to smoke. You shouldn't be allowed to sell cigarettes, period! Cigarettes should be illegal. That would put a dent in the health toll. It is amazing to me that we are an evolved culture yet we can still sell products to ourselves *that we know kill us* and we can rationalize it away. There is a government and a people and a society that all say this is okay. "I am going to do everything I can to get you to use this product that we know is addictive, that we know kills you." It's insane. It is the antithesis of the fundamental values of our civilization. Of course, the driving force behind this self-destruction is big money put to its ultimate use.

I find them bizarre, these lines we draw: It is acceptable to sell a product we know kills people, but you can't do it with a camel that looks like a penis head because that image is a little more appealing to a young person. "Don't get too persuasive. Sell death subtly, that's fine. If it sticks out and draws attention to itself, that's got to be stopped." This is why most cigarette advertising almost looks like wallpaper. The Joe Camel campaign was fresh and unusual, and maybe it was actually bringing in new users. That's what killed it.

I've never made a business decision, I've never promoted any product, I've never sold anything, where I have looked myself in the eye and said, "I can't believe I'm doing this." That doesn't mean I have to be in love with every product I sell. That's unreasonable. I don't have to think that Mitsubishi is the best car in the world to be able to sell it. I believe it is safe. I've had people say, "You're selling Snapple. That is not really good for kids; it's got sugar in it." I'm okay with that. We live in a world in which people drink soft drinks. It's not my job to decide whether kids are going to drink sugar products or not. I am not their parent.

A case could be made that through basketball, advertising is extending the influence of hip-hop culture and glorifying the screaming, taunting, in-your-face world of trash-talking, which some people take exception to. I see advertising as a mirror to society, and if you look inside the urban community's culture, trash talk is one of the ways the people there communicate. What you could say is that advertising captures the complete selfish, showboating aspect of the game and slam-dunks it.

But did advertising invent that culture? It did not. A segment of the African-American community, on its own, started a mode of communication that has extended far into the wider society. Is it the advertiser's job, or anybody's, to alter that? If it could be proved that trash talk leads to an escalation of societal violence, that would be a different story. I have a lot of problems with rap music that says "Kill a cop," because no matter how you slice it, that is foreplay. I don't pretend to be a rap expert, and cop-killing imagery may all be hyperbole and fantasy, but it sounds real enough to me.

There has been a lot of talk in the basketball world lately that one of the reasons so many foreign players are coming over and being successful in the NBA is that—rather than emulating the hip-hop showmanship that is seen in commercials and in the games and is highlighted on SportsCenter and is the goal of so many young American players—they grow up being taught fundamental basketball. In China and Argentina and Serbia-Montenegro they're passing, cutting, and setting screens instead of going one-on-one, hanging on the rim and hollering.

But that has nothing to do with advertising. They see the same ads everybody else does. If those players become more dominant and their teams start winning championships, you're going to see fundamental ball regain some of its dominance. Advertisers will reward the winners, and hip-hop commercials will give way to the next big thing, whatever that might be. It's the force of nature. When's that going to happen? When Dirk Nowitzki wins a championship.

Social responsibility should be the price of entry to everything you do. I fundamentally have a problem with the video games in which players—mostly kids—are encouraged to go on shooting sprees, pull people out of their cars by the throat and slice through them with machetes, so of course I have a problem with the advertising that makes these games attractive. I am not pleased with the entire genre of small-bottle, liquor-based soft-drink-looking products that are skewing younger and younger, being marketed all over TV. In fact in both the programming and the advertising on MTV there is a sexuality being promoted at a very young age—twelve, thirteen—that I have a real problem with.

I think we're riding into trouble with the whole world of "Jackass"-style advertising, the "Don't try this at home" stuff, people riding the hoods of cars. Advertisers do have a responsibility there. Television is one of the main ways many people connect with the world, and advertising that in any way shows anything unsafe that children could potentially mimic needs to be closely monitored.

Just putting a disclaimer on a wild stunt isn't anywhere near enough. I could argue that psychologically this is the same as encouragement; it's actually an appeal, almost a taunt. Disclaimer or not, when somebody does it at home and kills himself, your company can't say, well, we had nothing to do with it. You're responsible.

There are bad ads all over the place. Turn on daytime TV any day of the week and there will be hundreds of completely innocuous, one hundred percent invisible ads selling a vast array of products you don't take a moment to look at. Ads that you just don't notice. You don't even say, "That's so bad," you just keep on clicking. I couldn't name a one of them. In terms of tradecraft, those are bad.

But the worst ads? The worst ads I've ever seen? Ads for cigarettes, which kill you. Ads for video games that portray people killing for sport, raping for power, ripping out hearts, macheteing bystanders for points; ads that truly celebrate violence. I understand that violence is part of our culture, but promoting that is grotesque. I don't know how we as a culture look the other way.

The Risk of Not Being Risky

If you're not moving forward, you risk getting run over from behind. In advertising—as in all industries and organizations—something that is not risky can, in fact, be *more* risky because it will neither excite an old customer nor attract a new one.

You risk everything by risking nothing.

What is risk? It's the ultimate 360-degree conundrum. If you look at the companies in my industry who are known as risk-averse, traditional, middle-of-the-road, they're the ones actually in the greatest peril. They have been most vulnerable and their business has suffered the most. Many have gone out of business: the Bateses, the D'Arcys. Those agencies didn't bring anything new to the party. Sometimes you can bring scale, and you're so huge that size is what you've got going for you. You can survive on a massive distribution system. But if you bring neither monster scale nor incredibly brilliant product, if your offerings are not unique or smart or different, you become extinct. Over time, any company that does not create product that is fresh, inventive, challenging, stimulating—in a word, risky—is dead. That's the irony.

The big traditional agencies have consistently painted the upstarts as unreliable. "Boy, you never know what you're going to get from a Deutsch." That's always made me laugh. Truly, those agencies are riskier. I actually think that as a businessman I am very conservative and extremely risk-averse. Not taking risks in your creative work is a risky proposition. The work we do that others call "risky" we define as "different," "new," "unorthodox," "including the possibility of failure."

For Ikea, at first a fringe furnishings company with different kinds of product who was a new player on the block, *not* to do work that called attention to itself would have been risky. For Mitsubishi, a second-tier brand that didn't always have the best car and couldn't outspend its competitors, *not* to run with unexpected advertising would have been *extremely* risky. I heard, "Oh, man, you're doing all this New Age music and these kids are doing this weird movement and you're not talking about the car going from zero to sixty . . ." It would have been incredibly risky *not* to run ads that were outside the lines.

Zigging when other people zag is the price of entry for being important in anything.

Advertising, in many ways, is a business of sheep. The original idea, when it hits, creates herds of followers. It goes without saying, in advertising as in art, that the copy will not have the life of the original. I'm always looking for what I call the New Math—"What's the New Math?"—because when a company does something unusual, it tends to win more often than lose. For instance, live advertising. The first person who gets on the air and does live advertising is going to cause a big stir. The twenty-first-century version of "Now we're going live to . . . John Cameron Swayze for Timex."

We live in a world that craves new. Sometimes you get rewarded simply for the risk itself, not the quality of the work, if the DNA of your creation is unique. For years programming for television, the most dynamic medium in the world, was divided into news, half-hour sitcoms, dramas, or talk shows. Along came someone with a new idea: reality TV. Was it great? Was it compelling as art? Was it uplifting in any way? No, it was just a different critter, and it took off. And, of course, once it took off a caravan of followers took off after it. (That's hardly a surprise; from what I can tell, in the television industry you won't lose your job by running the third doctor show. The point is not to lose your job, as opposed to doing good work.) Somebody else took a risk and stumbled on the idea that people want to change their lives and now there's a makeover show in every world: houses done over gaily and straight, plastic surgery, life transformations.

People think creativity is the best version of the current thing. I disagree. I'd rather do something fresh and put my client on the line than knowingly do derivative work. Clients are smart, they'll go with me. I want something with a different flavor to it, the thirty-second flavor of Baskin-Robbins, the fifty-eighth variety of Heinz. New is Not Here Yet. I tell our people, "Go where tomorrow is. Let everybody else catch up."

I'm starving for satisfying advertising, and there's some good work being done. The new dynamic, the new creativity, is increasingly taking the form of how we're using the new media. BMW pioneered the creation of short films on the Internet, BMW Films. I don't know whether it's selling more new cars, but it's new math. Somebody's thinking.

Along the same lines, Target found a new twist on the day after Thanksgiving, Black Friday, the biggest selling day of the year. Everyone runs their early-morning fifty-percent-off sales, so Target ran an ad in which consumers could call a number and choose one of several bizarre options—from Darth Vader and Heidi Klum to a Latin lover to a hard-hat to Cheech Marin, a teenage diva, and a rooster—to give them a free recorded wake-up call so they could get to Target's sale on time. The videos were hysterical and the consumer could visit Target's Web site and run them again and again.

Target couldn't lose with something like that. The idea was fresh, and they got bonus points in consumers' minds just for thinking differently. I don't know whether it translated into more sales the next day, but Target made a statement about its brand that had to serve it well in the long term.

One of the best uses of new media was Burger King's brilliant subservientchicken.com, created by a hot agency in Miami called Crispin Porter + Bogusky. Burger King was coming out with a new chicken sandwich and, of course, was the home of "Have it your way." The agency came up with a guy dressed in a chicken suit and garter belt who would do anything you wanted. Go to the site, type in a command, watch the chicken. It's a riot. The concept was new and different and they got style points for the buzz factor alone.

For the most part commercials still fall into the same old types. There's the funny dialogue commercial, the lifestyle commercial, the product demo commercial. Unfortunately, in my industry there is a self-fulfilling prophecy. It's no surprise that widgets come out of a widget factory. Take cosmetic ads. Cosmetic ads pretty much all look the same: perfect face, perfect body, perfect skin, shimmering product. We tried to push the envelope with Revlon by creating small individual movies starring Halle Berry, Eva Mendez, Susan Sarandon, and Julianne Moore that were very beautiful but didn't focus entirely on the cosmetics. The campaign was unusual but actually still in the box, because cosmetics people believe you have to show the lips in a certain way and we did. Yes, I know you need to show beauty and you need to show aspiration. The religion of cosmetics is *You Have to Look Good . . . And You Can.* Yet the ads all blend together. Why can't we put a video camera in a woman's bedroom, or in her medicine chest at night, and talk to her as she's putting on her makeup? New Math. Risky. Too risky, apparently, for the world of cosmetics.

But sometimes circumstances can surprise you. Pharmaceuticals have broken out. For years all the antidepressant drug ads showed people in life situations, overwhelmed, afraid to get out of bed. Depression was stigmatizing. Instead of harping on people's anxieties, we created a campaign for the drug Zoloft that destigmatized the disease. We presented a series of very disarming childlike drawings that allowed people to engage. Our thinking was, Let's handle it like a child's lesson and do it in the least anxiety-provoking manner possible. Just tell people directly, "If you're depressed, you know what that feels like, we don't have to tell you. All that's bothering you is that some serotonin stuff is off in your chemical makeup. We can help." Hey, says the sufferer, it's not my fault! Instead of "Do you feel this way at parties?"—in which the prospective consumer is forced to relive exactly the symptoms he's trying to alleviate (the motivating factor being "I don't want to be part of that club")—we said, "Come here, sweetheart, we'll help you." Which would you prefer?

My first drill to everybody is "I want something completely different." I've got good people; it's going to be good, that's a given. But I set them free. I always say, "Let's fail miserably, that's okay. I'd rather go 'Holy shit, swing and a miss!' 'Oooh, bean to the head!' than snooze through something I already know how to do." I revel in pitching a piece of business when everyone else is in one place seeing the solution the same way and we're over on the far side with our own vision sitting by ourselves. I'm trying to make the world a fifty-fifty game, where it's us against all of them. If there are four agencies on one side of a pitch and us on the other, I've changed the game from four-on-one to one-on-one. I'll go one-on-one with anybody.

The Wayne Newton School of Product Polarization

It's better to have thirty-five percent of the people really charged up about you and the rest hate you than to have one hundred percent not care.

Who says universal acceptance is the answer to anything? Show me one product, one person, one idea that appeals to everybody. You can't. What you want to create, when you're selling a brand to the public, is a passionate constituency.

In the early '90s we were competing for the Tanqueray gin account. Their senior vice president, Nick Fell, was this James Bond–type chain-smoking Brit who was sent over by the parent company, United Distillers, to reconfigure the brand. Tanqueray's problem: the entire gin category was skewing older and Tanqueray was the number one offender. Among gin drinkers Bombay was hip, Tanqueray was old and WASPy, your father's gin. They wanted a younger consumer who would start drinking Tanqueray and not stop for a generation, so our brief was, How do you make the product hip but stay true to its roots? Tanqueray was a genuine brand with a distinguished history; if all of a sudden we ran a gin campaign and filled it with rappers, it wouldn't be credible.

The creative team was headed up by Greg DiNoto, one of the ramming-head crazy guys, and Kathy Delaney, now our creative director. Dallas Itzen was on the team along with a great art director named Patrick O'Neal. They were all very bright, some of the best creative people I've ever worked with, and two percent off-center, if not more.

The team came up with six or seven alternatives, then told me, "There's this one thing that you're just going to lose your mind on." They whipped out a picture. A gray-haired, imperious gentleman well into middle age, his face turned slightly into the camera, looked at me with austerity and reserve: the quintessential WASP gin drinker. His head dominated the page and the artwork below his neck was a stick figure in a tuxedo. He was holding a martini. They called him Mr. Jenkins.

The premise was, let's walk right into it. Instead of trying to pretend Tanqueray is what it's not, let's turn the world on its head and present Tanqueray for what it is, the authentic WASPy gin—and make it incredibly hip.

The campaign placed Mr. Jenkins in all these cool places interacting with the young crowd we were trying to attract. The graphics were goofy scenes laid out as elementally simple cut-and-paste collages with Mr. Jenkins's large head always the center of attention. The copy was dry, like a good martini.

At a dinner party: "Mr. Jenkins is encouraged that his suggestion to play 'no-handed pass the olive' is being received so enthusiastically."

At the opera: "Mr. Jenkins knows from personal experience that properly warmed up, the diva is indeed capable of hitting some very high notes."

At a pool hall (or in somebody's basement): "Mr. Jenkins demonstrated that a trick shot is more successfully executed when one sips Tanqueray martinis instead of pounding kamikazes."

The kickers: "How refreshingly distinctive" and "Do drink responsibly, won't you?"

It was like a train wreck; you couldn't not stare at it. It was very new math. This voice, this look, this hadn't been done before.

The client was incredibly taken aback. He was blown away by the originality of the concept yet frightened to try it because this was really out there.

We did a lot of qualitative research and in-depth testing with focus groups all over the country against three or four other campaigns and found that Mr. Jenkins was completely polarizing. People either loved him or hated him. Loved it/hated it. Yet at each hour-long session, even the haters were talking about Mr. Jenkins. He overwhelmed everything else, the concept was so compelling. We knew we had a pulsating campaign.

Most clients are so afraid of turning people off that they would have walked away. "A large percentage of consumers hate us? We can't have that."

But so what? If you're all things to all people, you're nothing.

Nick Fell and Tanqueray got it. Fell was one of the most courageous and best clients I've ever worked for. He and Tanqueray were brilliant enough to recognize what they had: a passionate constituency, a brand that a significant percentage of consumers would die for. You crawl over the moon for that.

There was just one problem. After the client fell in love with the campaign, Patrick and Kathy couldn't remember where they found the piece of scrap art they were using as Mr. Jenkins's face. We certainly couldn't launch a national ad campaign with the threat of an unauthorized-use lawsuit over our heads. Finally, after weeks of retracing their steps, they found the original—a society page picture of a Palm Beach socialite named Ridgely Harrison III. Perfect. And we couldn't have made up a better backstory: Harrison, our Mr. Jenkins, has left his wife—his second wife—for his third wife, who was his wife's best friend. He was the perfect real-life embodiment of what we wanted to communicate in this ad: a cad, yet certainly the kind of uncle you'd like to have a martini with.

Somehow Harrison agreed to let us use his likeness. I don't think he knew what he was getting into.

When the ad broke, it was a huge success. The people who hated it didn't buy Tanqueray. Who cares? They were never going to buy Tanqueray! The drinkers who loved it bought the gin by the tub. Brilliant client. Understood that the goal is to get people to love your product. It doesn't have to be everybody. It's not going to be everybody! That's genius.

The Hip-Hop–Sprite Syndrome

Life cycles and death spirals. What advertising can and can't do.

No one is unaffected by advertising. No one. Name a personality type, a member of a group, name a critter on this planet who lives in any part of modern capitalist society, save a hermit, and he or she has been moved one way or another. We're a product-driven world and I have yet to meet a human being who doesn't choose one product over another because of something he or she has seen, read, heard, been told about it.

Any time someone puts thought into his appearance, his lifestyle, we've had an effect. Obviously the people who buy BMWs rather than Mercedes have been convinced to see their purchase and themselves in a distinct light. But even nonbrand people, the anti-conspicuous-consumption folks—when they wear house brand Kmart khakis, they're making a statement. When they buy their Honda Element—a truly ugly car that looks like a child drew it up and was built to be a utilitarian box for people who don't care what they look like—they're making a brand statement. They're saying, "I'm above it all. I cannot be reached and I am smarter than the average consumer. My brain is my most appealing asset. My brain is my seduction tool."

But no, we know they're there and we're marketing to them, too. They're trying to make purchases that demonstrate intelligence and show an understated sense of materialism, so we emphasize intelligence and understatement, make those attributes our goal; we sell their brains back to them. It never fails. Any time they put thought into their appearance and then act on it, they become the same fashion victim I am with my Gucci loafers. They're making a choice and a statement; they're just wearing a different uniform. We sell all sizes.

But there have been changes. Today, people are more cynical about advertisers and advertising than ever before. They know more about the process and are more sensitive to the ways in which they are being encouraged to consume. People decipher messages differently now than they did twenty years ago; they judge the quality of the message as well as the quality of the product, and if one isn't up to the other, the advertiser can suffer.

Advertising cannot get someone to buy a product he or she doesn't want. What it can do is take a commodity and uncommoditize it. It can make any product, any thing, seem as good as it can be. An adept campaign can make a very ordinary deodorant, for example, seem extraordinary and get people to buy it for a buck and a half. When someone is prepared to spend six hundred dollars on a suit, advertising can get him into the store where it's being sold. At that point the product takes over. There's a classic saying: "The fastest way to kill a bad product is good advertising." If the public is alerted and the product doesn't deliver, you're done; they ain't coming back.

Advertising can also occasionally contribute to changing social attitudes. In 1992 we produced a series of commercials for Ikea in which people were shown shopping for furniture. The campaign's concept was that all lifestyles shop at Ikea, it's a store for everyone. Among the shoppers were an interracial couple, a divorced woman, people adopting a baby. One of these Ikea couples was two gay men. We didn't make a big deal of it; we didn't have "Steve" say to the salesman, "We need a bed for the two of us." We simply showed two normal-looking guys shopping for their home.

This was the first time a gay couple had been portrayed in mainstream advertising and we were aware that the campaign would generate a lot of media attention. That was fine with us; Ikea was a cutting-edge company that was all about inclusion, and increased mention of the Ikea brand meant increased sales.

We received an amazing number of letters from people thanking us for being so progressive. If we pushed the envelope a little forward and some gay man at home saw this domestic scene and felt, "Hey, it's okay to be gay," then the ad had an effect outside the economic. And inside—gays no doubt became aware of Ikea's calm acceptance of their business and patronized Ikea more readily as a result.

While advertising can on occasion affect social problems, it cannot fix a business that is fundamentally flawed. Sometimes there's just nothing you can do. Nonetheless, when business goes bad, advertising so often gets the blame. There are many businesses built on thirty- and forty- and fifty-year-old models that just aren't relevant today or haven't evolved with the times. The entire fast-food industry is in flux. Kids will always eat that stuff, but many adults have moved away from high-fat–high-carb meals for health reasons. Plus, there are only so many types of fast foods that taste decent and that people want to eat in inexpensive settings, and once you get past that, you run into problems.

Fast-food businesses have become irrelevant, overcrowded, and bad. Their infrastructures demand growth and they have become overoutletted, selling a variety of food that can't sustain that kind of expansion. In 2003, seventeen fast-food chains changed their advertisers. Burger King is a fast-food hamburger chain at a time when people aren't eating hamburgers the way they used to, and management hasn't been able to get past it. As a result, Burger King has been going through an agency per year. This is a classic example of agencies getting blamed when the fault lies with a broken business model. Seventeen agencies didn't get stupid all of a sudden.

People were saying McDonald's had lost it as a marketer, that their business was broken. But McDonald's turned it around. How? Not the "I'm Lovin' It" campaign. They fixed the business model. McDonald's started selling salads. Had they not introduced salads and continued to put their entire fortune in hamburgers, they would have continued going backward.

Subway's "Eat fresh" campaign starring Jared, the guy who dropped 245 pounds in one year, approached the problem from a completely different direction. They turned the concept of health food on its ear. What does Subway sell? Hero sandwiches. Loaves of bread with meat and sauce in them. Eat two of them every day and lose weight. It sounds absurd, but it isn't. Subway doesn't divide the world into them versus all the healthy food to be eaten; they divide it into them versus their competition: Pizza Hut, McDonald's, Burger King. When you line up Subway's sandwiches against other fast food, they are healthier.

The soft drink Sprite had a problem and they handled it right.

What was Sprite? The poor man's 7-Up. Someone very intelligently said, "Let's market this as a hip-hop drink. What have we got to lose? It's got no reason to exist, it's going nowhere, let's make it cool."

So they positioned Sprite as a cultural phenomenon. The ads

talked in code. "Obey your thirst" was a euphemism for "Stay true to your roots." Whose roots? Black roots. African-American street language in the campaign signified that Sprite was out of the mainstream, was not *Not 7-Up* but was its own definable self: Young Street People and those who followed them. And in marketing to blacks, they got the white audience as well, especially the young white audience—the huge young white audience that's buying the rap CDs and hip-hop clothing—to whom black culture and hip-hop attitude is the aspiration.

Sprite is owned by Coca-Cola. Coke has targeted the African-American audience for a series of ads over the years but has always stayed true to a larger place and bigger essence. While attracting and including the black community, Coke never pretended to be of it.

The Sprite campaign caught on and was very successful. The street bought it; the suburbs bought it; Middle America and the inner city had a new drink to share.

What would I do to get back on course if, sooner or later, Sprite were to falter? I'd say, "You know what? My brand was never about hip-hop. We're the voice of a young generation, and the underpinning of being young is always about rebellion, about being different. The important idea is to stay true to that voice. My brand was about being on the cutting edge, and hip-hop was cutting edge." What's the new cutting edge? What's the new in-your-face sign of rebellion for both the African-American and white communities? I'd find it and run with it.

There is a phenomenon now taking place that I feel is good for this country: The hip-hop community is starting trends that white suburban Americans, who want to be urban, are following in large numbers. The black community is taking hold of some great old white brands and making them theirs, and the cultural give-and-take that results is quite wonderful. As a result, for the first time we are seeing a truly integrated youth culture, a shared vision, a shared aspiration.

Some advertising understands that.

In 1999, Deutsch Inc. entered into a joint venture with hip-hop entrepreneur Russell Simmons called dRush, a youth advertising agency. We were going to bring together Deutsch's knowledge base and marketing expertise and Russell's intense contact with the pulse of the African-American community. But we did not succeed.

The problem was not in our concept but in its reception by clients. We could walk into pretty much any CEO's office with a proposal and present with confidence and style. Invariably they would tell us, "That's a good idea; we'll put it in the Af-Am budget." That niche ethnic budget was monumentally smaller than the one for the general market. Clients didn't understand that a hip-hop idea *was* a general market idea. We would commit staff time and resources, and if we did get the account, it was for maybe a tenth of what the same amount of time and energy would earn in other areas, so ultimately Russell and I had to give it up.

Nevertheless, any marketer selling to young people today needs to understand this black-white, chicken-or-egg relationship. Right now, it defines who we are.

The Business World

Women Are Muses

Thinking about sex? Good work.

I believe we are motivated in life by a single driving force—sex. Man meets woman, man meets man, woman meets man, woman meets woman—connecting with other individuals on an intimate, romantic, sexual basis is at the core of the human experience. Being attractive to one sex or another is what we're all about. To me, babes come with the formula, otherwise what's the point?

I don't think there's been a day in my business career when there hasn't been some woman at work that I fantasized about. People come by the office, look around and say, "Boy, the men and women at Deutsch are very physically attractive." Now obviously we hire supremely competent and talented people, but the idea of some woman that I'm excited to see or flirt with or even just think about stimulates me in business. I cannot remember a time in my career when I was not having either a flirtation with a woman in the office, or a friendship, a fantasy, or all of the above. I am at my best when women are there to energize and excite me.

Studies show—and if they don't, they're way off base—that the average man is thinking about sex a great percentage of his waking hours. Whether it's "I want to fuck that girl" or "Why haven't I fucked that girl?" or "I'm so horny," sex and how we appeal to the opposite sex—or the same sex, if that's your dinner choice—is a huge driver of everything we do. Whatever our universe of love is, we go all the way. The question "How is this going to get me into the sack" goes deep to the heart of all impulse to action. I truly believe that's why men accumulate power. I also believe it's the carnal guys who are better people and use their power to better ends.

We act shocked when we find that throughout history, men in power have been womanizers: FDR, Eisenhower, JFK, Bill Clinton. I would argue that this goes hand in hand with the personality type. Why do we expect men who are conquerors to stop conquering when it comes to women? If in ancient times you were conquering new worlds, or in the modern era you are buying up companies, why would that impulse go away? It's more surprising when things don't work out that way. Find me the sixty-five-year-old Master of the Universe who's still with his sixty-one-year-old wife.

Break this down primally, through history. Going back to the caveman, to ancient civilizations, what were the spoils of war? Beautiful virgins, the ultimate prize. Today, a guy's a nobody, then he makes money, which brings him power. What's the "in" thing he brings home? A trophy wife, the ultimate trophy. I would never want to be the dorky guy walking around with some hot girl who's on his arm for just one reason, but some guys don't care. "Yeah, so what? Whatever works. I got her."

We live in a world in which your material possessions, your stuff, increase your attraction. That's reality, can't argue with it. Why is this any different from a woman loving you in part for your looks or your sense of humor? If anything, a woman loving you for your accomplishments is more significant; looks were handed to you by genetics and fate; accomplishment is a function of who you are and what you have brought to the table.

Ask the expert, Donald Trump. There has always been a beautiful woman on his arm. (He is now happily married to the beautiful Melania Trump.) He uses charm, power, and money as aphrodisiacs. I was in a television studio when the Donald happened to be there taping an interview. Trump is everybody's friend and he started over to say hi. He was about five feet away and already had his hand out to shake mine when he noticed my assistant and an associate producer from my TV show, two incredibly cute women, sitting next to me to my right. I saw them register in his eyes. He exclaimed, "Donny!" and slid straight by me to the ladies, smiling, "Hey, how you doing?" It was a physical reaction; he couldn't control himself! I cracked up, they cracked up, he cracked up.

Trump is nothing if not consistent. We were shooting an episode of *The Apprentice* in the Deutsch offices. Night was falling and the women were in the process of beating the guys in that day's competition. They were working hard. Each one of these ladies was attractive in a different way. Large, small, leggy, busty, black, white—they had been cast well. Trump surveyed the scene. He was very much in his element. It seemed he had words of wisdom to pass along. He leaned over to me and said, "It's all about the babes."

The Client-First Formula

"What would I do if this was my business?"
How going over to the other side will better your own bottom line.

In all business relationships, in all buy-sell relationships, whenever a product or service is being bought by one entity from another—whether it's someone selling something on TV or a lawyer selling a position to his client—there is a built-in skepticism. When there is profit on the line, money and power to be apportioned, the potential for selfishness is always in the air. It is a barrier to be avoided if you want to do good business.

In advertising, the client is looking for two assets from the agency. They are both top-of-the-line; one is not more important than the other. Clearly the client is looking for the single item it cannot provide for itself: the creative idea. That's the currency of advertising; that's what they're there for. But equally important to the client—*equally* important—is the sustaining comfort of knowing that the agency actually has his best interests at heart.

Every client needs someone in the room—the head of the agency, whether it's one person or a group of people—who, at the end of the day, is his business steward; someone at the agency who is keeping the agency in check, someone who is watching his money. He needs to know that every single decision is being made based on whether it's right for the client's bottom line. The client needs an agency that treats his business as if it's their own.

At Deutsch, that person is our New York general manager and director of client services, Val DiFebo. A selfless woman and born leader, Val is a brilliant manager of clients. She is not only an extraordinary businesswoman and leader of people, Val is one of the most all-around delightful human beings I've ever met. She is one of six people who built the agency and she comes through every day. Recently we got great news; at age forty-four, Val had a baby. But being Val, the day after giving birth she was on the phone with the office, taking care of business. We had to tell her to take it easy, get proper bed rest, we'd handle things while she was away. She didn't want to hear it.

There is a healthy tension between clients and agencies. Creatives want to do the most advanced work possible. They want to be a force, to push and prod and drive their advertising toward breakthrough concepts. Theirs can be an emotional-innovational-commercial combo platter.

Clients want to sell the most product. Sometimes the two aims are not immediately compatible.

The client-agency push-pull gets danced time and time again. Where the real emotional bond forms, where relationships are developed that stand the test of time—because no matter how good you are, you're going to miss on an ad and need the occasional reprieve—is in that place where an agency executive truly becomes his client's advocate.

I wasn't always on top of this. I was at heart a creative for a long time and most of my impulses were toward letting my team run with the ball. It was only when I was forced to take on the role of CEO that I began to understand the full nature of the partnership.

My partner, Steve Dworin, was no longer at the agency and I was concerned that the clients that he had serviced might leave with him. One of the largest was LensCrafters, the national eyeglass company. The work we did for them was fine work—LensCrafters' eye doctors and their associates talking about how much they cared for their patients—but it was more conservative, more mainstream than we usually do.

LensCrafters was a good client and I didn't want to lose them. I was accustomed to selling ads to our clients using smarts and aggression—"We want to do the best creative possible"—but as I sat with them in my new business mind-set I wasn't at all concerned about how LensCrafters' campaign was going to look on our reel or how it fit in with our corporate image. I thought, "If LensCrafters was my company, what would I do?" That changed everything.

I separated myself from being an agency CEO. I went over to the other side. My main question became, and has always been since: "What is best for the client's business? If I were on the other side of the table, what would I be doing?" Once I answered those questions, I set about putting that information into practice. The work started to be about them, not about us. I wasn't simply going to make the client happy—there is a difference between informed advocacy and lapdog obedience—but I was going to think of my client's business before my own. What is best for your client's business? That is your God!

And it worked. With the true goal in front of us, our work became more focused, more defined, more effective. The change in perspective made all the difference. Today, we teach all our people that the first thing to do when you sit down to write a creative brief or develop an ad is answer the question, "What would I do if this was my business?"

LensCrafters stayed with us and thrived.

As the client meetings progressed I worked to develop a new rapport. Where I had always seated myself across the table from the clients during presentations—funny how I had never seen that as an implicitly adversarial position—now I began to sit next to them and across from our own team. I was a collaborator. I could whisper in the client's ear and they would listen. I became almost a liaison between us and them, and the distance between us began to shorten.

I changed the way we conceived of doing business. I tried to bring all the constituencies to bear. Pitching new business or working on day-to-day details, our mantra was, "If this was my company, what would I do?"

There is a lot of self-driven work in advertising, not all of it with the client's well-being as the primary goal; sometimes creatives just like to do stuff that's creative. While this may work on occasion, other times it comes off as self-indulgence. If you ask yourself, "Who's watching my money?" you're less likely to take wild and unsuccessful leaps. When they adopt this mind-set, creatives break down the natural barriers that do neither side any good.

And the bottom line was that we thrived; it turns out that by being about our clients, we ended up making things much better for ourselves.

I learned another valuable lesson many years ago from master public relations executive Howard Rubenstein. When I was young, perhaps only four years at the agency, I wanted to get some attention for David Deutsch Associates, so I paid Rubenstein and his organization a five thousand dollar monthly retainer, a significant amount of money for us at the time. A few months went by and I was not happy with the service we were receiving, so I went up to his offices to put him on notice. "This is bullshit," I thought. "Five grand and what are we getting?"

I began by complaining about how Joe, our account executive, was not serving us properly, and I gave Rubenstein detailed notes about what exactly was wrong. I expected Howard to try to dissuade me; that's what I would have done if someone came to me with complaints about one of my staff: defend my company and tell the client he was wrong. "No, you're really getting good service. Let me try and explain Joe's side of it."

Howard's reaction amazed me. He said, "That's unacceptable! I can't believe it's been going this way for you. You have every right to be angry. We are going to fix this thing right away! You know what, Joe's out. You won't hear from him again. We are going to put Louie on your business now. He's excellent and you will see the results."

What a salesman. It was his company that had fucked up, yet instead of defending the indefensible, Rubenstein had brilliantly separated himself from both the business failure and my anger and persuaded me to stay. It was his agency I was bitching about—his name was on the door!—yet he positioned himself as the problem solver. I walked in there prepared to fire him and I walked out feeling good. On top of getting improved public-relations service, I took home a fascinating lesson from a brilliant guy on how to run a service business. It's not about throwing your people under the bus. I'm sure Joe didn't get fired; he simply got moved to a different account. You want to defend your staff, but you want to be a step away so you can fix whatever breaks. You need to separate. Howard made me feel he was the guy watching my money.

The Learned-Helplessness Principle

Want to be a bad boss? Make every decision come through you.

Some organizations are so top-heavy, so dominated by one person's decision making, that they first become inefficient and then grind to a halt. This is a classic small-business disease. Want to be a bad boss? Make every decision come through you. Put down your staff's work in a rude or nasty way. Rule with such an iron hand that the people under you are cowed into waiting for instructions. This may fill an emotional need, and you may think you are leading by example. "If you want something done right, do it yourself." You're not. You are destroying initiative.

When mistakes are punished, not explained and then corrected; when credit is routinely denied and blame is constantly distributed; when things are intentionally broken so the boss can fix them; then staff would rather do nothing than get in the line of fire. Your staff came to their positions with some talent, some intelligence, some independent thought, that earned them their jobs. If your people aren't working properly, fire them; otherwise, let them do what they were hired to do. If you don't, instead of using their assets to solve company problems, they will sit there and ask, "What do I do?" That way they can't lose. They can't work but they can't lose. You haven't established discipline, you've taught them hesitation. You have created "learned helplessness." You sure you want to do that?

The Put-a-Stake-in-the-Ground Theory

Enough already. Give yourself time to do your best work.

An advertising pitch, like any situation in which a businessperson has to convince a potential client, is a jury trial. You want to prove your case convincingly.

It's always a good idea to brainstorm, to encourage all your people to use their best efforts to come up with the perfect concept. The freer the atmosphere, the better those ideas will be. But there's a timetable for good ideas; depending on the schedule, it's usually a matter of weeks, sometimes days. After that, if the creative meeting ends with "We're not sure" or if the boss says, "I don't like it; you've got to keep working," that's not good enough. There comes a time when you have to make a decision. We call it "putting a stake in the ground." You may not have the killer idea of all time; you may have one in five that seems to make sense. Go with it. You can win a piece of business without the best idea if it's brilliantly executed.

Let's say you have a six-week process; in the case of advertising, you're preparing for a pitch. You are better served by settling on an 8 idea in week two, putting a stake in the ground, and spending the next four weeks proving your jury case from soup to nuts than by waiting for a 9 idea until week five and trying to cram your preparation. At some point you have to say, "Here's where we're going—let's go! Let's put the troops behind it." I think that makes a statement to the client: We know how to lead.

A lot of agencies make the mistake of throwing ideas at the wall in hopes that one of them will stick and stick out. They'll present a series of unconnected programs, ready to flesh out whichever seems pleasing. "Here's idea number one. Here's idea number two. Here's idea number three." There's a moment of desperation as each concept flips to the top of the pile. They demonstrate no real conviction, and what is a pitch without conviction? If I am hiring a lawyer to plan my estate, I don't want him coming in and saying, "Here are five wills, you choose; whichever one you like, we like." I want certainty. I want polish. I want one idea developed to its fullest. Rather than divide our concentration, we focus it.

Sometimes a client will mandate, "We want to see three directions." We'll do that if we have to, but we never win that way; it's not our strategy; it's not the way we do things.

No, we'll present one idea. Even if the client doesn't think it's the greatest idea in the world, by the time they've seen it blown out across the disciplines in our kind of depth, they fall in love with it. Even if they don't immediately like the idea, the clients often say, "I love your integrated approach. I love the way you guys approach business. I love your thinking." Then, "Let's work on the core idea itself." By that time we've got the account and we're happy to oblige.

The Power of Managing Up

How to make your boss happy without being a total suck-up.

When you think of being a manager, of being *in management,* you always think of managing the people below you. How to get the best out of the people working for you, how to run a smooth organization, how to achieve your goals. Managing down. But there is an entire other element to management and that is the people or organizations above you. How to identify their real needs and satisfy them, how to communicate with them smoothly, how to help them achieve their goals. Managing up. The two are not dissimilar.

In dealing with a client I make it immediately clear who's the boss: them. We may sometimes disagree, and I will put my company's views and suggestions to them with force and conviction—fellas, that's why you hired me—but I will ultimately say, "Guys, it's your nickel. At the end of the day it's your call." I kiss their ring and respect their authority, but I also let them know that

I'm providing a valuable service, that we are an important asset to them as well. I often say, "We'll walk through fire for you as long as you understand that I've got a business to run here and I have certain needs of my own; we have profits to deliver. If you're respectful of that, I'll go through the wall for you." If they bridle, they're not the clients for us. I don't want to work for a bad boss, either.

I always judge the quality of a person by how he treats the people who work for him, not how he treats the people he works for; everybody treats the boss well. (As far as gender, despite the fact that I'm saying "he" all the time—this is the English language at work—you can replace all of the *he*'s with *she*'s; I mean to be genderless.) The worst kind of person, in my opinion, is wonderful with his superiors—whether it's clients, bosses, whoever is above him—and miserable to his underlings. Somebody who is miserable across the board, I can appreciate; he's made a choice and he's consistent. A toady and a tyrant in one, however, that's no good.

And there's no reason for it. I have met some powerful people and from what I can tell they all have one trait in common: they treat the president of the United States the same way they treat the security person watching the door. Dignity for all.

My father was the first to teach me this concept and I have gone out of my way to empathize with everyone in my own organization. When I walk into our building in the morning, I treat the elevator operators the same way I treat Linda Sawyer, our COO. I talk to them the same way and I relate to them in the same way. In fact, that's an important management tenet; when people see my evenhandedness, they get it and respect it. Our organization runs better as a result.

So I appreciate good clients and I enjoy working with them.

Of course, when you work for someone, there are certain liberties you cannot take. You can never be arrogant, that's an unaffordable indulgence. You can't be as flip with a client, for instance, as you can be with the people in your own office. Very simply, they are the boss. Obviously, at Deutsch I'm there to sell stuff for them and do good ads; that's a given. But there's always more. I ask our clients very clearly, "What are you trying to accomplish? What do you want to happen?" Again, I make it clear that their wins are important to us.

I also recognize that all organizations are made up of individuals, and I am particularly focused on what's a win for the people as well as the corporate functionaries.

"You're the marketing director of Mitsubishi, and yes, your job is to sell more Mitsubishis. But what do *you* want to happen? Do you want to become president?" This is a given: Their wins equal our wins. If they know that you're thinking about them in that way, if you have a set of shared goals, they will in turn care about you more. It's human nature. You also gain chits that way.

The Great Motivator:
A Good Firing

The weakest link is eliminated, quality work is rewarded, and the survivors feel better about themselves. It's a perp walk and sometimes you just need to do it.

The best manager is very much like a good parent, nurturing and demanding, loving but very tough. Your kids know you love them and that you have their best interests at heart, but you have standards they must live by, and if they don't, there's a price to pay. A great boss cares deeply about his entire organization and its individual people. He does not suffer fools gladly. Having said that, and not being a parent, I also find that a good firing can be one of the most motivational, uplifting tools around.

It's easy if someone is just screwing up totally. On some level—if you don't fire that person, if there is no accountability—leaving him in place is a demotivational tool for all your people who are banging their heads against the wall doing good work. They're going to sit at their desks and think, "Hmmm, this guy's not doing so great and there are no repercussions. Why am I making myself crazy working my heart out?" Then your office falls apart.

But in a more realistic world, if you have ten people working hard, nine achieving A's and one operating on a B level, and all of a sudden you yank Mr. B out and fire him, or punish him so severely it clearly causes pain, two things happen: One, the A students feel better about themselves. "Whew, I made the cut!" It validates the work they've done. They're now part of a more exclusive "A team" club. And two, they also know—if they didn't already—that anything less than A work is not tolerated.

Even if you get to a point where you as a boss have to make cutbacks of twenty or fifty or even one hundred people despite the fact that those people are doing their jobs and are losing them only because of hard economic times, while it is painful at the moment, the next day there is actually an esprit de corps that develops. The remaining employees, the survivors, feel better about themselves. "Even though those people didn't deserve to get fired," they think, "they certainly were the weakest. We're the best. We're still standing." They also think, "Got to keep at it. They're not going to tolerate anything but pure efficiency." As difficult as it may be at the time, somehow some good shootings are actually very motivational.

The same concept has been used in the legal system's handling of white-collar crime. You've seen it: The assistant United States attorney and a phalanx of federal agents arrest some high-level stockbroker for insider trading. They go to his office, confront him where he is most respected, cuff him behind his back, and with his tie undone and crisp white shirt only half tucked into his suit pants, parade him out of there. The film is on the evening news. No one's smiling. It's basically saying to the honest brokers, "You'd better stay honest," and to the dishonest guys who haven't been caught yet, "You'd better not do this anymore." That's what a firing is. Even though you never fire somebody in front of his coworkers, it's a public event. Everybody knows; everybody sees the guy clean out his desk. It's a perp walk and sometimes you just need to do it.

Despite my knowing that, one of my weaker management traits—though I've gotten better over the years—is that I find it difficult to fire people. I can scream at people, but to sit down and say to somebody, "You're not doing a good job. Here's why. You're coming up short, you're failing, you're gone," has never come easily.

The toughest time I've had firing people was when the job had outgrown them. We had a comptroller for a while, my chief financial guy, a very nice man. He came aboard when we had forty people in the organization. Certain jobs are self-contained. If you're a great copywriter, for instance, you're a great copywriter whether you are writing for a tiny account or a car manufacturer. By definition, almost by mathematical certainty, someone who is the right financial guy in a forty-person outfit is not going to have the same skill set needed to supervise an expanding business of a thousand. The job grew past him.

No one comes into your office and tells you the work's too hard and he wants to quit, but you never do anyone a favor by keeping him in a job that is over his head. When a person is overmatched and not performing, he can't feel good about himself. He knows the job is past him, but who's going to give up a regular paycheck in a growing company? Who can live with that?

Ultimately, feeling personally uncomfortable about doing what was clearly in the best interest of the corporation, I fired the man. Although it didn't feel like it at the time, I was doing him a favor; I forced him to find a situation that was more suited to his abilities, which fortunately he did. But if for some reason there's not another job out there, that's the natural order of things and you shouldn't interrupt it.

We had a head of field relations on the Pontiac dealer account.

Being a field guy is mostly about affability, customer relations, shaking hands. It's not rocket science. This was a really nice guy who had been with us a long time, and when the Pontiac dealers consolidated and fired us after many years on the account, I tried to find him other positions within the company, but we really didn't have a job that fit his abilities. By this time the man was probably in his early sixties and I was hesitant to fire him. "This guy's not getting another job," I told Linda Sawyer.

She said something terrifically smart. "Donny, if that's the case, you're enabling him to put off facing his future. Whether it's time to retire, whether it's time for him to figure out another career, he's capable of setting up the rest of his life. You're not his father and you're not helping him by keeping him from dealing with that." I kept him on for a year, but ultimately Linda enabled me to let him go.

And she was right. He was a bright enough guy; he figured it out. Our field guy changed careers and found work as a voice-over talent.

I fired a Deutsch Inc. partner. Actually, I told him he needed to find another job. He was a very bright man, he cared a lot, but he just couldn't play nicely with the other children. He was the kind of man who, if he had something that needed to get done quickly, would have an hour's debate about it. Clients would tell me, "He's a really nice guy and he's really smart, but we can't talk to him." He didn't understand that at a more senior level, ours was a business of people.

Finally I brought him in and said, "Look, I want this to work out for you. Here's the problem you're not realizing. I'm hearing it from clients, I'm hearing it from coworkers; you have to listen to me, this is reality: You're difficult to work with. Basically, to you everything is a black-and-white science: 'If the client wants to do it this way and I know it's best to do it the other way, we'll debate for as long as we have to and I'll win.'

"This is not a right-and-wrong game; there are a lot of gray areas. You have to accept that. You have to be somebody who people want to work with. Your job is to facilitate, not to debate it for four hours and prove that the client is wrong. You're the guy who's got to get it done."

After a lot of back-and-forth, I realized that he was a delightful person, his heart was in the right place, but he was who he was. He wasn't going to change his personality; he didn't want to and he couldn't. So, for the good of the company, he had to go.

This partner was not a man who deserved to be fired. You fire someone when they're inadequate or have failed; this man was working hard and giving the job his all, but he simply wasn't right for the tasks we needed of him. Rather than a dismissal, I gave him a time frame and told him to look for another job. He was spared the indignity of a firing and it was an easier way out for all concerned.

When managing people, it is very important to be able to differentiate the workable from the unworkable, remediable deficiencies versus personal limitations. For instance, if someone has been a wonderful creative and you want them to fill a more managerial role, you can teach them. How to motivate people, how to delegate responsibility and pass along credit—that can be taught. What you can't teach someone is drive. You can't teach sensitivity. Just as in basketball, you can't teach height. If you don't have it, you won't have it.

A CEO should never complain about his workers. I hear it all the time: "Oh, my people don't do . . ." whatever their failing. That boss is an asshole. Either he hasn't groomed them and grown them or he hasn't recognized their limitations and acted accordingly. Complaining is absurd; he should take stock of his training program or examine who he's hiring. On a social level, a parent who complains "My children aren't disciplined" is missing the fact that she is the person who didn't discipline them.

Some folks are capable of growth; others aren't. My father never understood that. We had a head of client services who was simply a passive person. My dad would say, "I wish Jim was more proactive. I wish he would be more aggressive." But if you're not an aggressive person at age forty-five, chances are you're never going to be aggressive. Some changes can be made, some can't. Negotiation techniques can be learned; crunching numbers can be learned. But you can't teach aggression any more than you can teach a sense of humor. You get what you get; you don't change people.

Whether your company is undergoing dynamic growth or not, I've found it best to be direct with people. I've also found, to my surprise, that people often do want criticism. If you can say, "Joe, you're not performing. You're coming up short, and here's why. Here's what's expected of you. You need to do this to succeed"—people want that! Direct honesty. They want feedback, even if it's negative; that's the only way they can grow and make a change. If you give people the opportunity and they can raise their game, that's perfect. The great people grow with you, and that can be heartwarming to see.

It's not your responsibility to make sure someone has a livelihood. Conversely, when somebody's working for you, their livelihood is your responsibility. If you're a caring person, a person of responsibility, you want to carry people—but that never works. If someone has to be carried, they're probably not the right person; they will be a drag on the organization and negatively affect the people around them. The only exception you make, obviously, is for reasons of health. I've done that twice, and both times it's wound up being not only good leadership but also good business.

We had a mid-level account manager, a good guy who was HIV positive and getting very sick. This was in the early '90s, before the sophisticated medical cocktails were available. His doctors had written him off; his T blood-cell count was at the point where he should have been dead already. He was dying. We kept him on for a long time because he was a wonderful man and I cared about him. I've got to believe most organizations would do this—if they don't, shame on them. Whatever it took, we were going to stand by this guy. Even when he was no longer able to work, we kept him on at full payroll, full benefits. I really couldn't do it any other way.

Unbelievably, the man responded to a new regimen of drugs. He became one of the poster boys for this new cocktail. By some miracle, he lived. I'm thrilled to say he's alive today and thriving.

I learned after the fact that our keeping him on staff had had an enormous effect on the morale of the entire company. I had not planned it, I had simply acted in the only way I found morally acceptable, but when people saw that we went beyond "Okay, this guy's not effective anymore; sorry but we have to get rid of him," they wrote it down in their check box. They went, "God forbid something happens to me, or the shit hits the fan, they're gonna be there. This is a good company." That goes a long way. People like to be involved with a place that has a heart. Particularly their workplace, where they often expect so much less. "This is a good place. These are nice people." That's important.

I never want to be the Scrooge scumbag in the movies, even if he's making all the right dollars-and-cents moves. I don't want to be that guy. I hear the same stories everybody else hears about violent, bullying bosses who throw things around, humiliate their employees, and rule by fear; the guys who have their creative teams present prospective campaigns, then slam the books down, scream, "This sucks," and walk out. I can never understand that kind of asshole behavior for two reasons: (1) Even if you're making money, you're a miserable human being. That's what you are; how do you live with yourself? (2) It's not good business to have people rooting against you. You fuck people and on some level they're going to find a way to fuck you. Yes, you have to be tough, and you can't be everyone's friend, but that behavior is not motivating. People don't go back to their offices and say, "I've got to do my best work for this guy."

It's common sense. Are you going to get the most from a spouse if you beat her? She might stay, but you're preying on her weakness. She's definitely not going to give you the best blow job you've ever had. She might even take a bite.

Look, it is a business, it's not a charity, but there is something beyond pure dollars and cents happening at Deutsch, something else in the walls other than "Okay, a buck minus eighty cents equals twenty cents, and that's our profit." Something else is going on here: our company has a soul. I think all great companies have a soul. I truly believe that.

Here is a business model that has served me well: Being a good human being is actually good business.

The Miles Drentell Doctrine, aka the CEO Electrochemical Equation

Sunshine, lightning, thunder. Enter any room in your organization and change the atmosphere.

I used to watch *thirtysomething*, the late-'80s television series about love and angst in a generation, just to see Miles Drentell. Played with malevolent dread by the actor David Clennon, Miles was head of the advertising agency that bought and then swallowed the series' lead characters, Michael and Elliot. He was smarmy, conniving, manipulative, and completely engrossing. (Some people say the character was based on the late Jay Chiat.) Miles was a great character, particularly for us in the industry who knew how close he was to the truth. Miles wasn't just doing advertising; he was creating a universe. He was eerily New Age and totally real-world. He was a big presence.

In one episode someone asked Drentell, "What do you do?" This was not an idle inquiry; most people didn't like Miles, he knew it, and he took the question for what it was, a threat and a challenge. He spoke in his Dracula-meets-Chiat voice and his answer was one of the most brilliant lines in TV history:

"What I do," he said, "is strictly chemical. It is reactive. I cause reactions."

The very key to management. You want to be a molecular presence connected to the DNA of your organization. Come into a room, a meeting, or even a conversation and the relationships change between the people and their work. Lift yourself out and there's certainly going to be a different formulation. Let them say your name and feel the atmosphere shift.

Your Own World

Do!

If you don't pursue your dreams you will, absolutely, never achieve them.

We all spend our time wanting things to happen. Wishing. It doesn't happen that way. You have to *do*. That doesn't mean you are going to achieve your goal simply because you pursue it; but if you don't, it definitely won't happen.

If I walked through the halls of Deutsch and asked each of the one thousand people working on the floor, "What do you want to happen in your life?" I'd hear a lot of stories. "I want to be creative director." "I want to open an antiques store." Meanwhile, they're working at their jobs.

Say you're an assistant at a brokerage firm; if you work hard, you'll make broker. If you're an associate creative director at an ad agency and do your job well, you will become a director. That's the natural vertical progression of things. I believe most of us, whether or not we enjoy what we currently do, have dreams that go further.

Dreams that will not happen in the natural vertical progression of things. If you're in the insurance business and dream of running a restaurant, you won't get there unless you *do*. What's the first thing you do? Go talk to somebody who owns a restaurant. "How much money do you have to raise?" You just have to go after it.

Your dreams don't automatically get answered. You have to do. Just *do!* Do or don't do, that's your choice in the world. Your success begins in your hands. If you're sitting in a cubicle working on advertising copy, or at a magazine churning out photo captions, or at a video store checking out DVDs, and you have a dream of writing a screenplay, go to the library and get a book on how to write a screenplay. When you've absorbed that, if you feel you need to, go to your first screenplay class. But sooner or later, start writing! You may not win an Oscar, but at least you are moving toward your goal.

I've dreamed about being mayor of New York City. Now, I have no right to be mayor of New York; it's certainly not going to happen if I continue to go about my normal day-to-day business of running an agency or hosting a talk show. I'm not an assemblyman, I'm not a City Council member, I'm not a district attorney; the progression is not natural.

But why shouldn't I be mayor? Michael Bloomberg did it. I'm a successful businessman, I know the streets, I care about people, I love New York, I'm a leader. I'd be a great mayor. As I've said before: Why not me?

What's the first thing I had to do? *Do!* I told myself, "I know this is crazy, but who do I know who knows somebody who is a political consultant?"

I called the guy on the phone: "Can I buy you lunch? Don't laugh at me, I know it's not likely to happen, but if I ever, ever, in this crazy vision, want to be mayor, what do I do?"

He did laugh. Then he said, "Well, crazier things have happened. First thing you've got to do is register for a 474 . . ." He started talking about the arcane but necessary steps you have to take to begin a run for mayor, and my dreams began to take a little more shape.

You can't be crippled by the fear of failure; that truly is the definition of not succeeding. If you do nothing, your failure is guaranteed. So—*Do!* You may write a screenplay that no one is interested in producing. But instead of treating this as an immobilizing failure, think of your success: You wrote a screenplay! How many people have talked for years about doing exactly that and have nothing to show for it? *Do!*

And you can't possibly fail. You are in a win-win position; even if you write and do not find an audience, you are still in the exact same place you would be if you didn't do anything. You have lost nothing. *Doing* is the ultimate win-win. So you failed, so what? You have succeeded; you have acted on your desire. And you can write another one, and another. The possibility of success is always there. So many people *want* but they don't *do*.

I have my own prime-time TV show. That's insane! Why do I have a television show? Because I can and because I *did*. One year earlier I didn't know I wanted a TV show. I had been a guest on a couple of cable productions, people had told me I'd done well, and I'd had a lot of fun doing it. So I thought, maybe instead of being a guest I could try the host's chair. That was never going to happen on its own. A lot of people are interviewed; pretty much none of them end up with their own show.

I asked around, talked to people I knew: "How do I get an agent?" I was an ad guy with a smart mouth, who was I even to think of getting an agent? Well, why not me? I found someone who thought I could be good and I said, "Let's go!"

CNBC and I found each other. We shot a pilot. How cool is that! If it came to nothing, so what; I had succeeded already.

There are five hundred channels on TV, so many different ideas and angles. I looked at them and, guess what, there were only two long-form interview shows: *Charlie Rose* and *Larry King*, both of whom have certainly been around a very long time. Television has a new and fresh version of every other type of program, from sitcoms to dramas to food preparation, but a contemporary version of the long-form interview talk show did not exist. No show with no band, just talk. Eighty thousand channels and it didn't exist. I took the lessons I'd learned from a lifetime in advertising and put them to use: less is more; do it different. Completely applicable.

The other concept I brought with me was the 1957 Boomer Theory: We are the generation that sets the pace and tone for the country and a good part of the world. I'd always done ads for myself; I'd figured if it pleased my sensibilities, then everybody else would like it as well.

I started with the set. There were legions of people who wanted to stay in the ordinary box. I found that amazing. Each talk show set looks the same: a desk to protect the host and give him some heft; and right up close a couch or chair for the guest. Rose has a round table; King, a rectangle. Always a barrier. Why? Because that's the way it's done.

Do it different! I sat in a chair in the middle of the studio; my guests sat across from me so we could check each other out.

The network wanted to put me in a crewneck sweater and slacks. I'm not that kind of guy. "You can't wear jeans," they said.

"Why?"

"Nobody wears jeans."

Ta-da!!

Nobody? Forget it, that's me, I'm different. And when you do different, it works.

The introduction's the same idea. Why don't talk shows open up with a smart piece of music instead of some cheesy piece of paint-by-numbers pop. I said, "Let me do it." So when our show opened, the audience heard Buddy Greco singing, "This Could Be the Start of Something Big." (It's since been changed to "To Be Real" by Cheryl Lynn.) It was different, it was simple, I liked it.

I went looking for the *duhs* of the television world. TV is compartmentalized. Talk show guests are stars with product to hype and they all have to make sense together. Anyone aimed at relatively bright, white-collar viewers is a talking head involved in politics, the entertainment industry, business. Anything that's stupid/silly is for blue-collar guys under the age of thirty.

Bullshit! If I went out with three bright, articulate, literate urban couples of any color, we would talk about politics, we would talk about business, someone would talk about their kids, but we'd be silly, too. We are not so refined that at some point either I or one of my friends wouldn't crane our necks and say, "Look at how hot that babe is over there."

Why can't the intellectual and the goofball live under the same roof? They do under mine. That was a *duh* for me. On my show I go from talking to Ed Bradley of *60 Minutes* to chatting with the yutz from *American Idol* who claimed he slept with Paula Abdul.

I began booking guests for myself! If I found someone interesting and wanted to talk to them, they were good guests. If I didn't, I didn't. Then I would talk to them on-air like I would talk to them anywhere I saw them, and about whatever pleased me. Matt Lauer of the *Today* show. Glamorous guy, Matt Lauer. Think about his actual life. "The alarm goes off at 4:10 in the morning; what kind of a life is that?" Hulk Hogan's daughter came out with a CD. He was warming up the crowd at all her concerts, got out there, ripped off his shirt, revved them up. I wasn't interested in Hulk Hogan the wrestler–media character, and for this moment neither was he; he was plugging his daughter. He was on my show as Hunk Hogan, stage father. Nancy Sinatra. She'd been all over the tube forty years ago and hadn't been seen much since. Did I want to know where she'd been? No. I asked her, Your father's arguably the coolest guy of the twentieth century; what was it like the first time you brought a guy home?

Because I like women, women and sex are a big part of the

show. Our first out-of-studio piece was shot at a bikini runway show. I was backstage interviewing bikini models, asking, "Which is harder, walking down a runway in a bikini versus the regular?" What a life. I was having fun and I assumed the audience was, too. Why can't you do that? Why can't you break down that wall between host and viewer? I was clearly having fun and the admission humanized me. That's important.

None of this would have happened if I had not acted on my impulse, my desire. I stepped outside the natural vertical progression and it paid off. I ought to put a plaque on my desk that just says, *"Do!"*

The Power of Self-Branding

Look around. What's the difference between exactly what you are doing right now and what you're capable of doing? The world will see you as you position yourself. Present yourself to your best advantage.

Let's just assume you're not quite where you want to be. It's a rational assumption; do you know anyone who is absolutely satisfied with his or her position in this world? Movie stars want better parts, business executives want more power and greater perks, middle managers want to be upper management, entry-level workers want to be in middle management, the unemployed want jobs. The drive upward is universal. How do you get there?

Create yourself as a brand.

How do you do that? First you have to say, "Why not me?" That's first. Lens it through your own eyes. You can never change your status, you can never change the way in which you are viewed, if you do not feel confident that you deserve the promotion. You must be secure in the fact that you deserve better. That's easier for some people than for others, but it's the basic prerequisite for advancement.

Once you have established that you are entitled to more than you have, you are in position to move forward.

The next question to ask yourself is, "What's my dream?" I don't know if there's anyone in the world—in any situation—who doesn't think she's capable of more. The question is, In what arena? I'm not talking about "I want to be a movie star." Given some realm of what you would call your best-case scenario, start with your *skill set,* draw a dotted line to *capability,* and from there to *"Where do I want to be?"* That's the goal. Then, to begin attaining that goal, ask yourself: What does that person look like? Feel like? Smell like? Taste like? How does he act? Where does she go?

The equation for successful advancement is entitlement plus self-branding. Who are you? What's the difference between exactly what you are doing right now and what you're capable of doing?

You can position yourself in several ways, all accurate. For instance: "I'm an ambitious, hardworking account planner for Deutsch. I've worked on many high-level accounts, I'm very smart, and I really want to pitch in."

Or: "I have worked with great success at Deutsch; here are my credentials. I am more than ready to be in charge of a division of your business—to be head of research, for instance. I possess leadership qualities that will allow additional people to work under me."

Both are correct descriptions. The first will lead to a parallel position; the second will land you a position of more authority and advancement. The choice is yours.

Once you are defined within an organization, it's very difficult to change your image midstream. The Deutsch human resources department interviewed a kid with an interesting book who was a receptionist at Chiat/Day. Why wasn't he interviewing over there? They would always see him as a receptionist. He presented himself to us as an entry-level art director and we hired him.

Linda Sawyer is the COO of Deutsch, my number two. Here are two pictures of her, both on the money:

(1) Chief Operating Officer, an incredible administrator. In an organization with a boss who has vision and a lot of jagged edges, takes up a lot of space, and likes the limelight, she is the great behind-the-scenes equalizer who makes the trains run.

(2) A woman who runs a $2.5 billion business who has driven it to the next level and is ready to operate a significant business on her own, without anyone standing next to her.

Both accurate. Which description she would present to a prospective employer—assuming, God forbid, that she ever made the unfortunate decision to leave Deutsch—would depend on how she wanted to project herself. Thankfully, Linda is comfortable doing what she's doing now.

Answer this question: "What is the clothing I'm going to wear?" I don't mean only wardrobe; I mean what are the external signals—the physical, social, emotional clothing—that you need to send out to be seen as the person you want to become.

For example, many people feel they are not being productive if they're not doing something tangible. They feel the need to be noticed, so they take notes. Don't. Look around. The decision makers, the more senior-level executives, are not writing. Other people write for them, so they can concentrate on the issues at hand. If you're a junior midlevel executive in a meeting with ten people, unless you are the person assigned to write the conference report and your boss is going to get in trouble if you don't, stop writing.

Don't carry an attaché case. When was the last truly important senior person you saw carrying a case? As a junior exec, of course, the first thing I bought was an attaché case, because I wanted to be viewed as serious. I didn't know any better. What was I carrying that was of such heavy significance? I had my *New York Post* and my bologna sandwich in there. (I think it would be a great social exercise to open people's attaché cases on the subway each morning and see what's really in them.)

If you want to advance, don't be afraid to ask for more challenging assignments. Do not demand. Request. If your job is to observe a conference, offer to write the conference report. If your job is to write that report, accept the assignment and say, "With all due respect, I'll write the report, but I'd rather be the one deciding the next steps in the meeting." At whatever level you find yourself, try to position yourself as part of the next tier.

Clothing counts. Years ago there was a very bright media supervisor at Deutsch who was in line to be promoted to senior vice president and associate media director. She wore unbuttoned work shirts and, every day, thong underwear obvious enough so it did not go unnoticed. I told her, "Andrea, you can still be casual, but if you want to be seen not as a media supervisor but as vice president, you have to carry yourself differently. Your physical appearance should parallel your responsibilities."

I certainly can trace my brand by the clothing I have worn during various stages of my career. Early on I wore a suit to work because I wanted to be taken seriously. Then, circa 1989 when I had established my credentials and I wanted to be seen as more of a renegade, I wore sports jackets with jeans and cowboy boots, now an embarrassing fashion statement but then kind of a half-and-half effect that mirrored my relationship with the business and creative worlds. After my falling out with my partner, when I took over the agency and needed to be viewed as solid and reliable, I took to wearing very conservative, very powerful, chalk-striped suits. When we finally gained a notable level of success, I figured I could do what I wanted—and the business community would be signaled that I would do what I wanted—so I started to wear very casual but stylish designer sportswear, open-neck shirts, and loafers. When we hit it truly big, I started wearing jeans and T-shirts, which is how I dress at home.

My brand and the company's have been almost inseparable. I have understood pretty much from the beginning that the Deutsch agency has a brand that some people love to hate. We walk our own path, we are not tied to convention, we speak the truth. People may not always like us, but the brand has always evoked an emotion.

My individual brand and the company's have mimicked my age in life. My personal brand for years was the brash, upstart Ad Guy of the Generation, the Bad Boy. It has stuck with me and now I can't get rid of it. Tomorrow I could take over Omnicom (the largest advertising holding company in the world), wear three-piece suits and be the most serious businessman in the industry, and I'd still be seen as the Bad Boy. I'd like to lose that, but I'm not sure I will. I accept the challenge.

When creating a brand for yourself, you can't forget your core competency. On my television show I'm trying to evolve into an overall media person, but at the same time I recognize that if I'm not an ad guy, I don't exist. Deutsch Inc. has also progressed while staying true to its core values, including ambition, aggressiveness, and our new business credo, "Leaner, meaner, smarter, faster."

Madonna never forgets her reason to exist; her brand is "cutting-edge sexuality." She came on the scene in 1984 with "Like a Virgin" and has evolved with the mores of the times. Whether she's voguing or kissing Britney Spears on the mouth on TV, as the cutting edge has changed she has stayed true to her core. Now she's writing children's books. If, instead of playing young, she can define cutting-edge sexuality as a cool, sexy, vibrant forty-seven-year-old woman moving through the next stage of her life—"Madonna as mother"—wow, that's staying true to your brand.

Why Hatred Is Good

If you don't have a natural enemy, you need to create one.

Think of all the problems in the world, all the true conflicts. They're not about religion, though these days it might seem that way; they're about the haves and the have-nots. That's what all wars are about and it has always been this way. Animals fight for turf; so do we. Go back to the caveman; you're in that cave, you see a shiny thing that some other caveman has—and you want it. "Wow! That's a shiny thing that person has. I would like a shiny thing, too!" It's very primal: "I'm going to get that."

As I've said, when I was growing up, money was not a defining issue. I didn't measure people by their wealth; money was not in the equation. I do remember my first day at Penn, meeting kids who had their own BMWs. I had strong feelings that day. I didn't feel envy; envy suggests that the other person has something that you *can't* have. Envy is a destructive, passive, defeatist emotion;

when you envy someone, you have already admitted defeat. Envious people don't win. Envious people are looking in from the outside.

What I felt was astonishment. The feeling that swept through me was: "Wow! I wasn't even aware that this shiny thing existed. Okay, I can have that, too!" It wasn't a zero-sum game; I didn't need for them to lose their cars in order for me to get one.

That's fine for civilians. But in business, very often, hatred is good. Hatred fuels empowerment. It's the ultimate motivator: you versus the world. You have to have someone or something that just pisses you off. It can be a person, it can be a company, it can be your parents' lack of faith in your abilities or the classic "They said it couldn't be done," but you need an enemy to prove yourself against. And if you don't have a natural adversary, you need to create one to use as inspiration.

I think it's a great idea to be angry. What could get your blood boiling more than to feel in your gut that your competition's success is unjust, that the situation—them above, you below—needs to be remedied if justice is to prevail. And justice must prevail! Hatred personalizes your drive.

In every field, in every endeavor, certainly in every business, there is a mountain and there are people standing on top of that mountain who personify success. Now, when you're new to a field, you're probably not going to invent the new gold standard right off the bat. The first thing you've got to do is shoot for it—blow the other guys off that mountain—and at the same time you're taking them down, work up your own standard of excellence. If you are in business, look at the next level of success, look as high as you can. If the fact that you're not at that level doesn't piss you off, you're not getting there. You've got to be fueled by the gut.

I'm a nice guy, I never want to see anybody else fail, but I do use other people's success to further my own ends. For example, I am hosting a cable TV talk show called *The Big Idea* on CNBC. Before I became involved in the talk show industry, Larry King and Charlie Rose weren't even on my radar. They had shows. Sometimes I watched. So what?

Now they piss me off. These guys are the definition of the long-form television interview. They are the best at what I do. I don't know Larry King and he doesn't know me, but he has a perch that I want. He books guests on his show that I haven't been able to book on mine, which translates into better ratings for him and his network, which is impinging on my success. I become irate. "Why did he get that guest? Why can't I have that guest? That's bullshit!" I listen to his line of questioning and think, "I could even do better!" and then construct my interviews differently.

Now, God bless him, I hear that Larry King is actually a lovely man. But in my mind, for my purposes, he's the enemy.

In sports, it's common to hate the enemy. The best prizefights, the best football games, are the ones where people say, "These guys really don't like each other." They gain motivation from that dislike. I think any great competitor has this trait.

On my show I asked tennis player Andy Roddick, "Do you ever see the competition as the enemy?" When he looks across the net, does he see someone specific? Is he trying to beat *that* player personally or does he just see a generic competitor with a specific set of strengths to handle and weaknesses to exploit? Roddick has something to look at now; Roger Federer has done a Tiger Woods and separated himself from the rest of the field. Andy said he just wanted to beat Federer the best way he knew how. Federer is clearly a superior technician, and whether Roddick likes it or not, there's a new gold standard. That's what Andy has to aim for now, and if he's going to reach the top, it has to drive him crazy.

The two best-defined brands in major league baseball are the Boston Red Sox and New York Yankees. You can tell them apart from a distance. The Yankees stand for the winning combination of quality and wealth. The Red Sox, you know what they stand for:

They hate the Yankees. That hatred is what drives them and it is exactly that hatred that got them to the Promised Land. Starting with the Curse of the Bambino and moving through Bill Buckner's legs to Pedro Martinez's Yankee "daddies," the Red Sox had more motivation to win than any other team in baseball.

And how smart they were to personify this hatred. The new Red Sox owners, after losing a bidding war for a prized Cuban pitcher, actually called their rivals "the evil empire." In one memorable phrase—like any good advertising campaign—they used national politics and popular culture to define the Yankees as a combination of the Cold War–era Soviet Union and Darth Vader! What better enemy?

The Multiple-Mountain Theory

Why I sold the business I loved and went looking for another challenge.

Not only do you need a person to shoot at, you need a good supply of mountains to climb.

Most people, if they find something they're really good at, keep doing it. For high achievers—doctors, lawyers, screenwriters, stockbrokers, businessmen—success at their level is difficult and rewarding. Why would they stop? "Wow, I feel good! I'm better than everybody else. I make all this money. I live well. Everybody tells me how great I am." If they're on a path, and it feels good, they stay on it. All of a sudden they're forty or fifty or sixty years old and they look around and find they've been doing the same thing their entire working lives. Maybe it's been fulfilling, maybe they don't even realize that they've stopped being passionate about work, that work has stopped being fun, stopped giving them plea- sure or excitement or satisfaction. Some people know they're bored, but many others have succumbed to the details of their jobs; they have worn the grass from the path and begun to feel as if they're just out there every day, slogging.

But this experience isn't limited simply to the high achievers. Everyone, from people on the loading dock to middle management to the boss, works to create a situation that is comfortable for himself/herself. We want to be comfortable financially, comfortable while we do our jobs, comfortable that "I know what I'm doing." Our goals are: "I don't want to work so hard. I don't want to worry about money. I don't want any stress." Rather than seeking out the sharp edges of challenge, we wrap ourselves in pillows and try not to get bounced around. It is a paradox, an irony, that we spend our lives working to create a place that, when we're finally secure in it, has had all the rewards removed.

Sometimes it's more interesting to blow it up.

I sold Deutsch Inc. to Interpublic Group of Companies, Inc. for close to $300 million. That's a lot of money, yet at several points during the time I was negotiating the sale, I became depressed. For me, the fun in work and life has been making sure I haven't gotten wrapped up in that pillow. I like elbows and hard edges.

Why was I selling? I didn't need to. I had a ton of money and was making more each year. We'd been Agency of the Year four out of the last five years and our annual billings were $1.5 billion and still growing. We were at our peak. Why was I doing it?

Because I felt I had won the game. Could we have grown the agency ten percent a year, twenty percent a year? Of course. I had my best ten years still ahead of me and our competitive advantage in the industry was only going to increase. I could have spent those ten years trying to double down. In fact, I sold the business and four years later nearly doubled our bottom line. If I had kept it going, I would probably have been able to sell for even more money. Though I thought at the time that I'd hit a financial home run, today I don't know if, long-term, it was the right pure-dollar play. What I do know is that it was the right life play.

If I'd kept and grown the company, the only new emotional get would have been the money. So I'd have more offices, I'd do more ads; all I'd be doing was putting a stack of cherries on top of my current accomplishment. There was no new cracking of the code. I wasn't feeling the same level of stress I'd grown to expect each day. I would walk into a two-hour meeting and know how it would come out an hour and forty-five minutes later. There would be twenty people in the room and I'd want to conduct the meeting in a minute and a half because I knew where it should end up, where it would end up, and how to get there rapidly.

I like to make a difference. I like to be heard. That's why I enjoyed working on a presidential campaign, why I like doing television. What could I accomplish for my sense of self, my ability to effect change, by going from $300 million to $600 million? At that level the money is only about keeping score; my life wouldn't change at all. I didn't know it at the time, and I've had several years to think this through, but one of the things I was doing by selling was forcing myself to find another mountain.

Sometimes, instead of you forcing yourself, life forces you. I have a friend who'd been a salesman for technology companies for a good part of his adult life, until he got laid off. Forty-five and out of work, a troubling time. What does he do? His first impulse was to look for another tech sales job, but the industry was in a freefall and those jobs were scarce. I said, "You're a salesman. A good salesman. Doesn't mean you have to always sell technology. Maybe it's time to create that new mountain." He brightened. He'd never thought of it like that.

Within the structure of what they do for a living, the way people get the best from themselves and stay vital is by creating new challenges. I don't mean you should hop from career to career, but if you feel your enthusiasm flagging, you should do whatever it takes to rejuvenate and interest yourself. For my friend it was the concept that, rather than being closed out of one industry, now every industry was open to him. For me it was a cable TV talk show.

As host of *The Big Idea* I spend a considerable amount of time trying to figure out how to connect with people, how to attract good guests, how to get high ratings. I'm in the process of figuring out internal and external television politics. I'm still in very uncharted territory. I have my own talk show, which is a triumph in itself, but my show is a very little item in the scheme of things. I'm not a big TV name, I don't have security at the network. I do have the luxury of not needing this job; my livelihood does not depend on it. But in some way my sense of myself does. I'm working hard to succeed. It's exciting! The work is fresh and exhilarating, the mountain is in front of me, I'm climbing it—I will be successful!—and I'm feeling more alive than I have in years.

The Charles Atlas School of Business Theory

The power of knowing you can kick everyone's ass.

Masters of the Universe—those extremely successful people who move and shake and shape the destinies of businesses and cultures and countries—spend their lives trying to make money, amass power, and control the world. But as I said to my buddy Miramax's Harvey Weinstein over breakfast, "What good is it being the top guy in the movie business when you're so not in shape? This is the one thing you can control. What fun is it knowing that all the chicks want to sleep with you for one reason only? Takes the fun out of it." I was kidding around and Harvey, to his credit, cracked up. (I'm not saying it's because of what I told him, but Harvey has since lost a ton of weight, looks great and has never been happier.)

So many things in our lives are out of our control. The most important element you can control is your physical well-being: your weight, your strength, your conditioning. Not to do so is true insanity. If you're in shape when you get sick, you will recover more quickly; if you're in shape, you may not even get sick. The more successful I've grown, the better shape I've gotten in. I don't want the external world to be attracted to me simply because I have money or notoriety, I want people to look at me and say, "Man, that guy's got it together."

Being in shape makes you better in business. If you're in a meeting, at a conference, around any business roundtable, it's nice to know that you can physically take whomever you're doing business with. Of course that's never going to happen, but it's an emotional state of being and, I think, a very compelling place to work from. It's visceral. Adds tremendous confidence. It does truly help me; it's just nice to know that if things get out of hand, I can kick his ass. That's a powerful tool. (I'm kidding, sort of.)

Obviously, it's never going to come to that, but I have on occasion threatened to punch people's lights out. Guys have talked to my staff disrespectfully and I've said, "If you open up your fucking mouth again . . ." But more than in actually popping somebody, there is incredible power in the ability to sit at a table and know "I'm strong."

"I'm strong."

What more do you need to know? That image of yourself extends to all areas of your professional and personal life. Physical well-being says you are disciplined, you are a winner.

How did this dawn on me?

In 1992 my partnership was splitting up, I was in a bad marriage, and I was five foot ten—a Jewish five foot ten—and 220 pounds, more than I'd ever weighed, in my life. I was unhappy and food was my only pleasure. After I ended that marriage and settled the partnership, I said, "I'm taking control of my life."

By 1997 I was down to 195 and had been going out with a woman for several months. We went away for the first time together over Christmas. To Florida. Beautiful Boca Raton. We had a fight one night; she was fooling around and flirting with another man. She had run into a few fellas she had gone to college with, and, unbeknownst to me, on the other side of the pool they'd said to her, "What are you doing with that fat older guy?"

I probably wasn't consciously connecting the dots—I mean, I hadn't heard them take me apart; she only told me about it years later—but something must have drifted my way. I *was* that fat older guy and I didn't like it one bit. When I see fat older guys with hot babes, I don't envy them; I think they look like idiots. The next day I said to her, "My New Year's resolution this year is to get in shape. I'm going to call a trainer."

I didn't want to walk into a gym where everyone else was in great shape and I'd have to learn how to use the machines, so I asked around and found a place called Definitions, on Madison Avenue in the eighties, where people looked like I did and the training was one-on-one. Not a muscle gym. I showed up and the boss looked at me and took one of his trainers, Michael Givens, aside. He said, "I've got a real project for you."

Michael and I worked hard, and sooner or later I began to come around. I'm now in the best shape of my life, I've lost forty-five pounds total, and eight years later Michael is still my trainer.

Fitness goes plateau to plateau. You have to keep pushing it, just like in business. You move upward, you level off, maybe drop back a little, then move up again. Progress is not straightforward; it's an overall line that keeps advancing at an angle upward. At first you take baby steps—it took me seven years to go from puff to buff—and if you told yourself it'll take seven years to complete the journey, you might not start. So you say, "I want to feel a little better," and you lose the first five pounds. The first time you get two big plates off your chest on the bench press it's a miracle. Your shoulders widen, your waist trims; your stomach stops jiggling when you brush your teeth. You notice all this and it makes you feel good.

And you enjoy your successes. If I looked now like I did after two years of working out, I'd be disappointed, but at the time I felt like a champ. And I continue to work out. Two years from now who knows what I'll think.

I have a picture of myself with then-Governor Bill Clinton taken on the campaign trail in 1992. I'm pudgy in my open-neck shirt, I'm grinning, I've got a head of big hair; Clinton has his arm around my shoulder, solid, clear-eyed in his suit, smiling. I have another picture with Clinton, taken twelve years later. In this one I'm trim, muscular underneath my T-shirt and sport jacket; my hair is close-cropped, I look younger than I did a decade earlier. Clinton is still smiling, but he's grayer, fleshier, more worn; looks like he's been president for eight years.

This sounds like a silly, goofy theory, I know. But pain or paunchiness can render you almost helpless. If most of your energy is being spent keeping you upright, it's not going into the areas where you need it most keenly. Go to the flip side of that equation and you'll see how being in tip-top shape can help you immeasurably.

I love the fact that most of the time when I'm with my contemporaries I am the most physically tuned. Makes me feel stronger than they are—not superior but more confident. A top guy at CNBC, Jonathan Wald, turned to me over dinner one evening and said, "How do I get arms like that?" Made me feel great. "Work out five days a week!" I told him. "It's simple."

But time is going by and as I age there's only so much I can do. No matter how hard I work, I'm still going to be a little soft; I'm forty-seven, I don't have a twenty-seven-year-old body. Still, there are choices. Some men give up on a certain element of their lives. "You know what? I'm a dad and that's the most important thing, so this is the way I look," they rationalize. Or, worse, "I'm married." So they become married soccer dads and they go to seed. But you can still be a great soccer dad and not give up on your body. Guys say they don't have the time to devote to it, but I don't buy that crap. Think of your workout as a meeting with an important client: yourself.

I schedule my workouts for eight in the morning. You can schedule yours whenever it's convenient, but you need to treat your sessions with respect. The temptation, when an associate says he wants to meet you at eight to talk business, is to think, "Screw it, it's only a workout." But if someone said, "I really want to meet you at eight," and you already had a client meeting you'd answer, "I really want to meet you. I can't do it then; let's get together at ten." Time gets figured out, it just does. You wouldn't cancel one client to talk with another, and who's a more important client than you?

I'll say it again: Strength and physical well-being are vitally important in business and in life.

Now, if I met a guy my age who was in better shape than I was, it would piss the shit out of me. I'd have to go back to the gym and work harder, press more, take it up a notch. Don't want this guy kicking my ass.

The Big-Shadow Principle

The greatest brands aren't for everyone. They have an impassioned constituency that really buys into what they do. Nike is about being your best self, Starbucks is "the third place," Ralph Lauren is classic American aspiration.

Same way with agencies. Same way with people. I'm a very conciliatory guy. I wouldn't have success, our agency wouldn't have its successes, if I didn't understand how to get along with people. One of my favorite business phrases is "What's a win for you?" If I can find out what my clients want and then give it to them, I figure I've had a good day. But I also understand that you're not going to play in every room, nor do you have to.

I've always approached Deutsch Inc. like a brand. There are certain clients who say, "Oh, Deutsch is not for us, they're too aggressive," or "Donny takes up too much space." And part of the problem the agency has always faced is that I do cast a big shadow. We spent a lot of years early on convincing people, "No, Donny is not that much of an asshole." (I hate it when people talk about themselves in the third person, so let me quickly say it wasn't me who had the tough sell of telling potential clients that I wasn't a jerk; that thankless task fell to the people around me, and they did a hell of a job. Then I'd show up and try to live up to it). Even today, people obviously understand the depth of the agency and the cutting edge of our work and the quality of our players, but we still suffer from "Ah, that arrogant bastard." We always have a very clearly defined product, which is us, but sometimes I really do make it harder for us.

In 2002 Deutsch had been named Agency of the Year by *Adweek* for the fourth time in five years and by *Advertising Age* for the second time in that period. This is a very prestigious award in the advertising world; it means you're the best at what you do. It's coveted. Advertising cares about this thing. For a while, I did, too. But by 2002 part of me had gotten a little numb to it, didn't have the same level of appreciation. I wasn't proud of our industry. Deutsch had outdistanced its competitors but being on top was unsatisfying because of the low level of competition. So when a reporter from *Ad Age* came around, I was awkward about telling the same story again: how wonderful we are, how great our work, how devoted and talented our staff. How many times can you sit there and tell your business philosophy to an audience that already knows it? It's fair to say I was bored with our success.

It must have showed. After a very short time the reporter said, "Come on, Donny, we can't write this again. What have you got that's interesting? What's behind the scenes? What's the big news?"

I don't know what got into me. Maybe I'd been out late the night before, maybe I was bored, maybe I just wanted to bite the hand that was feeding me so well. More likely it was my way of saying, "We're past this award. We have climbed that mountain. It's not even exciting anymore. We're bigger than that." Which was arrogant but not without merit.

It didn't hurt that the reporter was a woman.

"I'll tell you what the real story is," I told her. I pulled my white T-shirt off over my head and started flexing my muscles. Mind you, I was pretty buff at that point. I'd gotten divorced, I'd just lost forty-five pounds, I'd been working out every day like a maniac, I was in fact looking pretty damn good. "The real fucking story is, I have the best body of any advertising CEO in the world! See?"

I was obviously kidding around. I was being silly, I thought I was being ironic and self-deprecating. I was being an idiot.

The reporter laughed, I laughed, we laughed together.

This wasn't a new occurrence around the office. I'd been known to take my shirt off before. Goofing around, showing off, lightening the atmosphere so people were in a good mood and good work got done. "How'm I doing?" That sort of thing. It was an ongoing joke, part of the two percent off-center culture of Deutsch.

When *Ad Age*'s photographer came up, I did it again, as a goof, but told the magazine they could only use the shot if I let them. I thought it was funny. When the magazine called asking permission, I ran it by my staff. Kathy Delaney and Linda Sawyer looked at me like I was insane. I knew this was going to start an ad-world fire, but part of me said, "You know what, I just want to do it to say, 'Up yours.' " For some reason the staff didn't think this was a sound business decision.

As much as I wanted to tell the industry what I thought of it, and as protected as I was by both position and wealth, I ultimately realized that I was responsible for the well-being of my partners, my company, the many people who lived at Deutsch. I was at a stage in my career where I could afford to take chances and take whatever might come at me, but if it was going to negatively affect these people—for whom I had not only financial responsibility but real affection—then I couldn't do it. We argued fairly loudly, but finally I saw the light. So, no pictures.

I should have known there's a difference between taking my shirt off among friends and colleagues and doing it in front of a reporter. Sometimes candidness, a certain goofball lunacy, a willingness to let people into your world and have some fun, just backfires. It certainly did this time.

When the article came out, instead of including the caveats "sophomoric attempt at self-deprecating humor," "wink-wink, nudge-nudge," "he said laughingly," the reporter wrote it straight! "Donny Deutsch makes a fist with his right hand and flexes his bicep. 'I have the best body of any advertising CEO in the world,' he says proudly. . . . His bravado, some call it arrogance, is deeply ingrained in the agency's culture."

And everyone who read *Ad Age* that week got the same impression: This guy's a fucking asshole!

That was bad reporting, but shame on me for allowing her the opportunity. It was wrong for a hundred reasons. Maybe I was trying to get a little attention for a new career I was starting to forge in television; maybe I was, as absurd as it sounds, bored with all the success. Maybe it was just a brain fart. Whatever the motivation, it wasn't right for my partners, it wasn't right for the agency. Plenty of CEOs flex their muscles in public; they just don't take off their shirt to do it. I was selfish, stupid, self-destructive.

And now it follows me around, it's part of my résumé. People Google me and find that article and it's part of my permanent record. "Donny says . . ." It's the perfect lead. Sometimes you're a wise guy and it backfires on you. Sometimes you just do schmucky things.

Strength Sells

Powerful leaders will test you. They respect strength. The last thing you want to do in their presence is fold.

Extremely powerful CEOs—this being the real corporate world, they are still almost invariably men—are usually surrounded by people who tell them what they think they want to hear. Power and money are intimidators, and most people tend to bow before them. But these guys are no fools; they know when they're being flattered, which is almost all the time. When they find someone who is not afraid of them, who will talk directly and give honest counsel, they usually pay special attention. They're so happy to have someone to talk to. When you get past the bluster, honesty is the currency these people value. Now they value you.

I've only met one CEO who didn't want to hear it, who didn't want to be told he was wrong. After a single meeting with him, I said, "I'm never going to work with this creep." I didn't care how big the account was; it was a relationship that was doomed. Why bother?

We did a campaign in 1991 for the National Cable Television Association. This was when cable was under siege; they were going to be bought out by the phone companies and needed to convince the public that the delivery system was great. Ted Turner was on the organization's board and I met him.

Years later Deutsch was brought in against a handful of other agencies to pitch CNN, which at the time was still owned by Turner. The site was his conference room in Atlanta. It was the ultimate toy box. In this room you had the Atlanta Braves' World Series trophy, you had the *Gone With the Wind* Oscars, you had the America's Cup, you had the MGM lion. For a guy brought up on American popular culture like I was, this was a staggering collection of icons.

We were sitting around a big conference table, maybe twenty people in all, when in lurched Ted. Something was up. I didn't know what planet he was on. He came in and growled, "Hey . . . how's it goin'," then plopped himself down. I was introduced. "I remember you," he drawled, "you're the guy with the Gucci loafers. I remember you." I didn't know if this was a plus.

My creative director Greg DiNoto stood up and began his presentation. About ninety seconds into it Turner said, "That's the biggest piece of shit I've ever seen." There was a pause. "But go on."

Greg didn't miss a beat. He was completely unfazed, he was on top of his game, and he nailed it. Turner respected that. When he wasn't able to get my guy to buckle, he sat back, listened, and we got the gig.

The same human principles work up and down the ladder. You forget that sometimes when you're dealing with a very big-time person. Don't. You must show them respect, but it is vital to deal with the powerful in a straight and honest way. What you're saying is, "I'm as strong as you." That's what they want to hear. You can step into their sandbox now.

Most companies run by big monarchal figures tend to be difficult, and Revlon, run by Ron Perelman, was notoriously more difficult than most. Very bright, incredibly demanding, Perelman had a reputation that preceded him. Revlon was in trouble at one point, they felt their agency wasn't doing a great job, and Ron wanted to bring us in. He gave us one project to start, we aced it, and all of a sudden we were put in charge of all their business.

We got the account in the morning. At five that afternoon Perelman called the office looking for me and I wasn't there. He told my assistant, "I need to call him at home. I need Donny's home number." She gave it to him. He called my home. "Where's Donny? Can you beep him?"

"I don't know where he is," my wife said.

She knew where I was. It was Tuesday night and I was playing my regular weekly basketball game with my friends. When I got home she told me the story.

The next morning I called Perelman back.

"Ron, I love you," I began, "but you don't have enough money in all of your bank accounts to make me your account executive. That's not what I do. I can't do my job effectively if I'm up in your office every day. I will run your business. I will be your guy. Tell me what you want done and I promise you I'll get you there. But you've got to let me do it my way, the same way you run your business; then you and I will be partners. But I'm not coming up there showing you ads three times a week."

What I was saying to Perelman and what he took away from our conversation was, "We're peers. I'll walk through fire for you, I'll get it done for you, but I'm not the account guy. I have people who do that. Let me run my business." Ron respected that and we have had an extremely strong relationship ever since. He is one of the most brilliant businessmen of our time. He has become a mentor and a very good friend. We speak every few weeks. He knows I'm the guy to call and say, "Donny, that stuff sucks." And he knows I'll tell him exactly what I think.

What happens when you create this kind of scenario with someone above you on the business food chain? You win three battles. Number one, you're coming from strength and you will earn respect as a result. Number two, you're not taking up all your time tending to minor details, which allows you to free yourself to do the real work necessary for your client's well-being. Number three, you're setting up a situation in which you're in a position to fix things. If I had jumped when he called, I'd have been jumping all the time forever, I'd have become part of the problem. Positioning myself as the fixer, I could from then on come in and get my arms around whatever was bothering him, which is what a provider in a service industry does. You need to deal from strength in all service or selling scenarios.

Part of the reason I started dressing casually at the office, aside from the fact that it made me comfortable, was that I realized there was a charm in my implicitly telling clients, "I don't have to dress up for you." I was never going to be inappropriate; I wasn't going to meet with a bank in jeans; then you're just an idiot. But there was a message I was sending: "We're that good." On the flip side, when I'm working with junior people who might be tempted to defer to me, I constantly try to make myself accessible. I'm more at home that way, more likely to give my best, and so are they. If I'm sitting in a room with someone who's afraid to voice an opinion, or who's treating me with kid gloves, we're wasting our time.

Fact is, this translates into the social world as well. Guys, when you go on a date, do you want the girl who tells you from the beginning that she is going to do right by you? No, you don't want desperation; you want a woman who knows she has a lot to offer, who is being charming and connecting with you but has the self-respect to think, "Well, I'll do fine for you, but what are you going to do for me?" It's got to be mutual.

Got a blind date? Trying to impress? Don't be the auditionee, be the one holding the audition. If you walk in with the mind-set "Of course this person is going to like me; the night depends on whether I like them," it's amazing the good things that can happen. Your date will feel your confidence. "This person must be pretty special if they can have that attitude and still be nice about it." You control the dynamics and you can take that night wherever you want it to go.

The Next World

Got Rich, Let's Go for Famous

It's a club. Whether you're a movie star or a politician or a TV personality, when you've got the patina of celebrity, people treat you differently than if you're just another rich guy.

What a country. The difference in public interest between celebrity/notoriety and wealth is fascinating. My company has created advertising that's been seen by almost the entire nation; we have spent twenty years affecting the buying and consuming patterns of millions of people; I sold that company for a quarter of a billion dollars: I have actually, without their knowing my name, had a significant effect on the lives of many people. When I'm introduced as "Donny Deutsch, he built a three-billion-dollar business . . ." people are kind of impressed. But when they hear "And he was on *The Apprentice* . . ."

"*You were on* The Apprentice *?!*"

Whatever your world, attention never hurts. Whether it's celebrity, notoriety, or a combo platter of the two, if you have the opportunity to get some, grab hold. If you're in the insurance business and you win the Insurance Guy of the Year Award, spread the word; it can only help your business. If you're a deli owner in a small community and can sponsor that Little League team, do it. If you own a deli and fought off a stickup man, find your way into the local paper. There are ten delis that customers can walk into; they're going to want to talk to the guy who stuck it to an armed robber; they're going to want to tell their friends, "That fella on the news? I talked to him." How many people walk into Rupert Jee's Hello Deli because they've seen him on *Letterman?*

There are two business lessons here: It doesn't pay to be a shrinking violet. It pays to know those who are known.

Walk into the spotlight. If it's not in your nature, find a way. You've got to be who you are, you can't play anyone else's game, and there are successful people who don't want that kind of attention and fly under the radar. I'm clearly not one of them. But remember, attention is a tool. Use it. I don't think there is a downside.

Linda Sawyer, our COO, is evolving into Deutsch Inc.'s CEO. She is not a spotlight person. She's happy sitting in the background making everything run smoothly; that's her personality. She and I are yin and yang. In the office, though, she's a hoot. Very strong in her opinions, very articulate, very funny, and extremely able. I have pushed Linda to get out there and present more of a dynamic public persona because, as I am stepping to the side to spend more time on my television show and will be less visible in the advertising industry, our business needs that presence from her. Over the years she has told me, "I don't like that. It's not me." But the expansion of her profile has now become the right business move, and for the good of the company she has taken on this role.

And it has been working. There was a Q & A with Linda in the *Wall Street Journal;* she has started getting involved in industry functions and speaking to industry groups.

There've been two results. One: As I knew she would be, Linda is terrific at this kind of work. Any fool can see she is a strong, talented, engaging woman. And two: She's enjoying it! Her picture shows up in *The Wall Street Journal* and all of a sudden she's dressing better; she looks the best she's ever looked. "It's kind of fun, isn't it!" I told her. She agreed that it was.

So beyond the fact that it's good for our business, she forced herself to enter a new phase of her work life . . . and she's loving it.

A 1993 article in *Adweek* referred to me as "MaDonny." They were taking a shot at me, of course, equating me to Madonna, in that I was everywhere and very well known. But I don't see how that's a bad thing. In our little ecosystem of marketing and advertising, I was a celebrity, and people want to be near celebrity.

Over the years we've taken a lot of criticism along the lines of "Oh, Deutsch Inc. gets so much attention. Donny's a PR hound . . ." I just think that's smart and good business. It says to a client, "We know how to brand and market ourselves and clearly we can do it for you."

We are a velvet-rope society. On some very basic level of the human psyche, we all want to be behind the velvet ropes in one form or another. I made the Deutsch offices, the Deutsch world, into one big VIP room. I want clients to feel when they come to us that they have gained membership in a club. That's our brand: the coolest club. The product is hipper, the prestige is greater. We have some velvet ropes around us.

And we're not alone. The great lawyers send out signals of exclusivity. They have their mystique, their notorious or sensational or highly inaccessible clients. The "best" doctors operate on the most notable people. If you've got all the money in the world, you must have access to the best of everything, right? People want in.

In an absurd cartoon version of reality, Procter & Gamble's Mr. Clean ran a "Getting-to-Hard-to-Reach-Places Sweepstakes" in which the grand prize was a walk on the red carpet before and admission to the after-party following the People's Choice Awards. This is the American Dream come true.

Why do people flock to have their picture taken with celebrities they don't even know? Walk into a billionaire's office and he may have pictures of his wife and kids on his desk—maybe—but I guarantee he won't have pictures of himself with his best friends who are also billionaires, unless they're well-known billionaires. Depending on his culture level, he's more likely have pictures of himself with Roger Clemens or Richard Petty or the president of the United States. It's a club—"Look at me, I have access to that club"—and the initiation fee is fame.

Money helps.

Michael J. Fox has a brilliant line about life at his level of success: "Rich and famous is great. Rich is great. Fame without money is the worst thing in the world, because you're standing waiting for a bus and people are coming up and bothering you."

I'm on television, but I'm not a star; I'm some guy with a talk show. I'm at the stage where I love it when people recognize me. If anybody walks up and tells me they like my show, I couldn't be friendlier. I suppose you can have too much of a good thing, and I know that some celebrities keep their head down rather than make eye contact and have that awkward "I notice you noticing me" moment, followed by the endless line of autograph hounds. But my show certainly works to my business advantage. The ad industry is not a business that trades on celebrity, but now when someone says, "Donny Deutsch is my ad guy," as opposed to Joe Blow who may be equally competent, my client feels a little better about himself because at his cocktail party he's got a story to tell and friends who will say, "Yeah, I saw your guy on TV."

It works in my life as well. I've spent twenty years building a business, riding and jockeying an important agency to the top of my field, creating an environment in which a thousand people make a living. That's a lot more impressive to me than getting my mug on the tube. But the trappings that come with making a lot of money and being accomplished in business pale before the fairy dust that showers upon you when you're in show business, and it certainly has some appeal. Ever since my show went on the air, I've been getting the front table at restaurants, and when I sit down and the conversation begins, all people want to talk about is: "What was Yoko Ono like?" "Is Carmen Electra as hot in person?" "Is Jack Welch as brilliant as he seems?" Everybody's interested.

I was having dinner with some of my pals from Penn, all hugely successful, very smart, and powerful money guys, each worth hundreds of millions of dollars. I usually prefer to deflect the conversation from my life to theirs, but my interview with Yoko Ono had aired the previous day, so the conversation naturally turned my way. She's a cultural icon, she had an impact on my generation and me, and I'd met her. No one in that crowd had access to a Bee Gee's wife, nor a Beastie Boy's, let alone a Beatle's.

With this TV attention, new doors open to me. Fairly or unfairly, they do. And what comes with it is a new pool of interesting people at a new round of high-profile occasions. These are not important parts of my life, but I can't deny that it's fun to have access. I end up in social and business situations interacting with some of the most interesting and powerful people in the world. And that is a nice outgrowth of my success.

It's a club. Not a rich club: a fraternity of people who share celebrity. Some of them were nut jobs to begin with and went after fame as a goal; others got it in those rare moments when their abilities dovetailed with the public's interest. Whether it's a TV personality, a well-known businessperson, a movie star, or a politician, these club members treat me differently now that I'm on television than they did a few years ago when I was just another rich guy.

Which means only so much to me because I've never been impressed with celebrity. Accomplishment has always been my goal. I've got friends I've known since fifth grade who have lived good lives and done good things with them. Some have made a lot of money; others have gotten by. All of them are Queens famous, remembered in the neighborhood with great affection. Those are the people who impress me.

But what the fuck do I know?

Index